George H. Boker

Königsmark - The legend of the hounds and other poems

George H. Boker

Königsmark - The legend of the hounds and other poems

ISBN/EAN: 9783743303331

Manufactured in Europe, USA, Canada, Australia, Japa

Cover: Foto ©Thomas Meinert / pixelio.de

Manufactured and distributed by brebook publishing software (www.brebook.com)

George H. Boker

Königsmark - The legend of the hounds and other poems

KÖNIGSMARK

THE LEGEND OF THE HOUNDS

AND

OTHER POEMS.

BY
GEORGE H. BOKER.

PHILADELPHIA
J. B. LIPPINCOTT & CO.
1869

CONTENTS.

	PAGE
KÖNIGSMARK: A TRAGEDY	7
THE LEGEND OF THE HOUNDS	159

MISCELLANEOUS POEMS.

COUNTESS LAURA	183
THE FIDDLER	195
AD CRITICUM	199
DIRGE FOR A SAILOR	203
ISABEL	205
A DIRGE	207
SONG	209

PATRIOTIC POEMS.

OUR HEROIC THEMES	213
CAPTAIN SEMMES	224

CONTENTS.

	PAGE
CAVALRY SHERIDAN	229
FORT FISHER	232
ODE ON THANKSGIVING DAY	238
HYMN FOR THE UNION LEAGUE	243
SONNET	244

KÖNIGSMARK:

A TRAGEDY.

DRAMATIS PERSONÆ.

ERNEST AUGUSTUS,	Elector of Hanover.
PRINCE GEORGE LOUIS,	His eldest son.
PRINCE MAXIMILIAN,	A younger son.
COUNT PHILIP KÖNIGSMARK,	Colonel of the Guard.
COUNT VON PLATEN,	Prime Minister to Ernest.
BAUMAIN,	Captain of the Guard.
PAGE,	To Countess von Platen.
SOPHIA DOROTHEA,	Wife to Prince George.
COUNTESS VON PLATEN,	Favorite of the Elector.
MADAM WREYKÉ,	Her sister.
COUNTESS VON KNESEBECK,	Maid of Honor to Sophia.

Lords, Ladies, Guards, Attendants, etc.

SCENE: Hanover.   TIME: 1694.

KÖNIGSMARK.

ACT I.

SCENE. *A Hall in the Electoral Palace.* *Enter* COUNTESS VON PLATEN *and* MADAM WREYKE.

COUNTESS VON PLATEN.

In love? I doubt it. If you mean by love
That rare, unselfish passion which confounds
The sage's logic and the poet's art;
That sweet religion of the heart which makes
Martyrs of men and saints of women. No;
Once in a century the aloe blows;
Once in a century humanity
Is topped by such a flower. He is a man
Less likely to affect a single woman,
Because so readily impressed by all.
Trust not his pliant nature. You may mould
The treacherous clay to any shape; the gem
Takes but one form, and keeps it.

MADAM WREYKE.

How is this?
A month ago he was your paragon,
Your flower of constancy. If Königsmark
Were false to you, to love, to anything,

KONIGSMARK.

Then Nature lied through all her catalogue,
And earth, air, ocean and their multitudes
Were one stupendous fraud!

COUNTESS VON PLATEN.

Yet he was false.
When I believed most, I was most deceived.
He acted—there's his secret—he portrayed
All that love should be to my listening heart.
Poor fool, that stormed applause at every scene;
Laughed at his humor, at his pathos wept,
And thought his mimicry was real. At last
The curtain fell; and I went out of doors,
Into the midnight, desolate, alone.
He used me for his ends. Upon my heart
He set his foot, and vaulted into power,
Reckless of that which bled beneath his spurn.
What office holds he that was not my gift,
Wrung by hard labor from the grudging hand
Of the Elector?

MADAM WREYKE.

You forgive him?

COUNTESS VON PLATEN.

I!
I hate him deeper than I dare to tell.
Day after day his Countship trips me by,
Decked in his feathers, Colonel of the Guard—
Prince Max's friend, Prince George's friend, the sage
Who gives the Elector counsel o'er his wine—
This man whom I created! Or, perchance,
He stumbles on me in a corridor,
With a light laugh, "Ah! Countess, is it you?"

He who could see me farther than the hawk,
As you were saying, not a month ago!

MADAM WREYKE.

What will you do?

COUNTESS VON PLATEN.

I know not; I have no plan:
There's a wild fury beating in my breast
That must and shall have prey. I'd calmly sit
And see his heart bleed, drop by drop, while I
Counted each drop and droplet as they fell.
Torture! there is no torture that could do
Justice to my full hate. I can believe
That he aspires to win Sophia's love ;—
What virtue is there that he would not dare?

MADAM WREYKE.

But he may fail.

COUNTESS VON PLATEN.

He shall not. Through this girl
I'll be his ruin. And Sophia, too;
I have scant reason to bear love to her.
My lady's virtues are the Court's new cry.
All the light dames and graceless reprobates,
Whose time is taxed to dodge discovery
Of their own slips, rain satire on themselves
By lauding her. She is a minster screen,
Behind whose holy blazonry the choir
Make mouths at heaven, while their accorded throats
Join in its praise. Even the Elector—heavens!—
A man upon whose soft and waxen youth
Vice stamped the counterfeited seal of age—

A knave in folly's service, who has worn
Her tawdry livery till it hangs in rags
At his sharp elbows—he takes up the cry,
And preaches virtue, as though Heaven had made
His wicked lips its mouthpiece!

MADAM WREYKE.

                       One may see
The issue of all this.

COUNTESS VON PLATEN.

                    Yes; I shall be
A waning moon, setting before her rise,
Unsphered, dishonored, out of time and place,
Scarce marked by any in her blinding light.
She has become the Elector's dearest care.
He rates Prince George for his neglect of her;
Takes counsel from her; and the courtiers,
So quick to see where royal favor shines,
Huddle to the bright spot, like unhoused doves,
And strut, and coo, and trim their ruffled plumes
Beneath her smiles. Ah! if Sophia knew
What wings they have, for a tumultuous flight,
At the first shadow!

MADAM WREYKE.

               If Sophia knew?
Shall she not know? It seems to me your power
In Hanover was stricken with decay
At her first coming, and it needs but time
To dwindle you to nothing. You may urge
Your husband's post as minister, your own
Long hold upon the Elector's heart, your rank,
Your skill, so often shown in state-affairs,

As pledges for your safety. But you know
A minister may change within a week,
A favorite in a twinkling.

    COUNTESS VON PLATEN.

      True enough.
I have been shaken, but I keep my hold;
And where this foot is planted, there I'll stand
Against all Hanover. Count Königsmark—
Ha! ha! you see how he comes up again,
Just like the Vice in the old mysteries;
Turn as we may, we cannot shake him off—
He has a hankering for Von Platen's place;
And people talk of him; he has his clique:
Sophia, too, will doubtless lend him aid
At the right moment. Things look fair for him.

    MADAM WREYKE.

Let his plot ripen—

    COUNTESS VON PLATEN.

      Let it rot, I say!—
Drop, blasted in the blossom! Let him plot;
But give me leave to watch him at his work,
And shape the issue of his plots for him,
And he may rack his cunning. How he'll stare
When all his schemes come tumbling on his head!—
Roof, column, cornice, not a vestige left
Of the brave mansion into which he wrought
His pride and wisdom through such hopeful days!
He has gone far enough.

    MADAM WREYKE.

    But how to check him?

COUNTESS VON PLATEN.

With bit and bridle, as you check a horse.
You'll see mad capering, restless flings and bounds,
But I shall tame him.

MADAM WREYKE.

                I am glad to know
That you have taken these affairs in hand.
I was concerned about you long before
You broached the matter. I was full of fear
Lest you, in blind security, might miss
The threatening omens which I plainly saw
Rising around you.

COUNTESS VON PLATEN.

              Sister, I have eyes.—
In proof of which, I see Sophia coming
Fresh from the garden, whence her grace has stolen
Pinks for her cheeks and violets for her eyes.
Airing her virtues for the general good,
And purifying Hanover, no doubt;
Or taking in a stock of holiness,
Of the last mintage, as it fell from heaven
In showers of sunlight. Or perchance, and worse,
Count Königsmark has flushed that pretty face,
And the bloom lingers though the Count is gone.

MADAM WREYKE.

I met them yesterday. He strode beside her,
Bearing her boy into the palace door.
A mighty lump of babyhood that boy;
And the Count panted with the double weight
Of it and his own dignity. I laughed;
And asked if that new duty was among

His many cares as Colonel of the Guard?
He mumbled something out about Sophia
Being fatigued, or faint, or lame, or ill,
And frowned, and passed along.

COUNTESS VON PLATEN.

     Ha! gone so far!
But one step more, and who can sound the depth
Of the steep ruin into which he falls!
Why, after all, my dream of love was false;
There is but one thing true, immortal hate.

MADAM WREYKE.

Let us retire: the Princess comes this way.
          [*Exeunt.*

(*Enter* SOPHIA.)

SOPHIA.

I wonder if the crocus is in bloom
At backward Zell. Here they have violets
In plenty. They, I said; not we, but they:
I cannot learn to call this place my home.
Despite the ceremonious parade
That, by one act, divorced from Zell the hand
It gave to Hanover—despite the claims
Of wife and mother, and the harsh rebuff
With which my father disavows his blood,
And bids me look to those around me here
For comfort—I am still a stranger. Still
My truant heart haunts round the wonted home
It fears to enter, dreading stern rebuke,
And sobs, and sighs, and wistfully complains,
Hugging the door-post which it dares not pass.
I know not why it is. If I compare

Poor Zell with wealthy Hanover, I shame
My frugal home. But, ah, my heart is blind,
And is not dazzled though my eyelids wink.
So, to my partial vision, Zell appears
A paradise, and Hanover—well, well,
At least a purgatory; for through it
I hope to reach my paradise again.

(*Enter* Königsmark.)

Philip, I was just thinking—

KÖNIGSMARK.

Let me guess.
You were just thinking of dear Zell. I see
Regret and love contending in your eyes;
Tears that drown smiles, and smiles that brighten tears.
Do you remember on a day like this,
When we were children, ere your rank had raised
Your heart so far above poor Königsmark,
How we would hunt the crocus in the fields;
And finding one—ay, but the first pale leaf,
Pushed just above the sod—we clapped our hands,
And cried, "The Spring is come?"

SOPHIA.

You read my mind:
'Twas of the crocuses at Zell I thought.

KÖNIGSMARK.

Yes, of the crocuses; but you forgot
Our rambles after them.

SOPHIA.

    That I confess.

    KÖNIGSMARK.

Ingrate!
    SOPHIA.

 Why so?
    KÖNIGSMARK.

    Am I not all that's left
Of Zell to you? I am the only pledge
Of all the treasures you have left behind—
The only link that now remains to you
Between your cradle and these days. Am I,
Whose eddying life ran side by side with yours,
Through its first dewy hours, too poor to bide,
Even as an alms-man, in your memory?
Ah, Princess, Princess! Yes, that titled name
Is clue to all. You have climbed too high to see
Down in the misty valley whence you came.
But I, from my low stand, can trace your path,
Counting each footprint; and no less exult
To see you glorified upon your height,
Though far beyond my reach.

    SOPHIA.

   You wrong me, Philip:
You know me better than to judge me thus.
You would not hear another so belie
Your friend.

    KÖNIGSMARK.

  My friend! Friend is a solemn word;
But, like most solemn words, of easy use.

    SOPHIA.

I do not use it thus. To you alone

The dangerous secrets of my life are plain.
Before your sight I lay aside the mask,
In which I play this comedy of life,
And show you that the tears which crowd my eyes
Are not of mirth, but sorrow.

    KÖNIGSMARK.
    You are homesick.

    SOPHIA.
Homesick for Zell, but sick of Hanover.
Had I no other refuge, I would hence.
This hollow mummery—this cold, stiff life—
This playing princess to exacting crowds,
Too dull to praise, but all alive to blame—
Palls on my taste. I am besieged by hate.
For every friend, I make ten enemies.
Even the Elector's smiles come back to me,
Reflected from a thousand jealous eyes,
In sullen frowns. The Countess gnaws her nails,
Sneers at my little wisdom, mocks my taste,
Wishing my virtues, which the Elector lauds,
Were safely housed in heaven.

    KÖNIGSMARK.
   Have you no more?
What of Prince George, your husband? Have you
  learned
To bear his insults and neglect with smiles?
Can you be courteous to his favorites;
And ask their intercession for such boons
As he denies to you? When we begin
To jostle through a crowd of things like these,
We soon grow sore or callous.

SOPHIA.

          Hush, Königsmark!
There are some mysteries of a woman's heart
That even friendship has no right to touch.

KÖNIGSMARK.

Now, Heaven forgive me if I slander him!
I thought his deeds were patent. Ring your bell,
And call your lowest scullion from her fire;
Ask her to name Prince George's mistresses,
And you shall have a list to make you stare.
Why, even with me, will you deny this shame,
Or pass it by in silence?

SOPHIA.

          Why will you
Still press the subject as though I were deaf?
Can you not be contented with my pain
Unless you hear my cries?

KÖNIGSMARK.

          Ay, shout aloud!
Wake Hanover, wake Heaven, wake George himself,
Ere you submit to this degrading life!
That which you think your goodness, men have made
Your just reproach. You foster and maintain
Your lawless husband in his vicious ways
By your tame conduct. Trust me, there's more sin
In conscious apathy than erring acts.

SOPHIA.

What should I do?

KÖNIGSMARK.

    Do nothing, as you wish;
Else would you ask for counsel?

SOPHIA.

    Königsmark,
Woman's long lesson is submission; we,
Kindly or sternly, are compelled to know
That the world's shaped by larger hands than ours;
And our one task is to adapt ourselves,
With our best skill, to forms we cannot change.
You launch us on the tide in gilded boats,
With silken hangings fluttering over us;
You tug and strain to row us smoothly on,
And while we smile, your work is ecstasy;
But let us venture once to touch the helm,
And the whole crew rebels. An idol waked
To actual life and motion, by the zeal
Of those who worship at some pagan shrine,
Would scatter the devout in wild affright:
So we poor women, we poor stocks and stones,
Sit on your altars in our painted rags,
Dreading to lose our feigned divinity
By the least sign of life. You nettle me,
Knowing my anger is of no avail.
You thunder manhood in my shrinking ears;
Bid me pick up my distaff as a sword,
And lay about me like a Paladin!
I am a woman, Philip.

KÖNIGSMARK.

    And for that
You're to be trampled in the mire! To-day

I saw you standing by the Elector's chair,
When your sweet husband with his latest prize,
Tall Ermengarda, flaunted into view.
I gazed, the whole Court gazed, in dumb surprise,
Upon your face, to catch a righteous frown,
A sneer of high contempt, a twinge of pain—
Looks that would so become you, as we thought.
We saw them not. Heaven's deep serenity
Was rage to your composure. In dismay
Each looked into his neighbor's vacant face;
Then toward the doting couple turned all eyes,
Flaming with the disgust you dared not show.
Ay, the most shameless losel of the Court
Took up your cause, as if it were his own,
And made the indecent monsters feel the shame
Of their bare-browed iniquity.

SOPHIA.
     I saw
The general stare, the general look of scorn,
And thanked my God for his supremest work—
The daring, noble, holy human heart!
Think you, if the broad brand of the whole world,
Laid hissing on his forehead, had no power,
That the weak murmurs of an unloved wife
Can wake a feeling?

KÖNIGSMARK.
    'Tis not for his sake.
No! I'd not put a straw across the path
Between him and perdition. Let him go,
With all his wantons trooping at his heels,
To make hell merry. But for you, in whom
My pride was centred from my infancy,

Who are a second and dearer self,
I would demand more deference and regard
Than the punctilious duelist who seeks
Occasion for a quarrel.

SOPHIA.

                You are kind,
Dear Philip, you are very kind. I blame
Your actions towards me often, but, oh, never
The heart from which they spring. I have a
    scheme—
The only one in which I'll bear a part,
Even against this heartless libertine:
'Tis this: to fly from Hanover, to quit
A shameful evil that I cannot cure.
Once in security, we'll talk of terms;
Or leave my husband to what course he likes.
Zell and my father's heart are shut to me;
He would return me faster than I came,
Giving my husband warrant, by the act,
For baser usage.

KÖNIGSMARK.

              In the Court of France
I have good friends. Or Dresden—what of that?
What do you think of Dresden?

SOPHIA.

            I would go
Among my kindred, and stop scandal's mouth.

KÖNIGSMARK.

True, true! Ah! there's Duke Anthony.

SOPHIA.

               Well thought!
He loved me ever.

KÖNIGSMARK.

            I will find some cause
To ride to Wölfenbuttle, and acquaint
Duke Anthony with your sad history.
He hates this Hanover from end to end.
They ousted him from the Electorate,
Broke the betrothment 'twixt his son and you,
And, worse than all, laugh at his anger now.
I'll work it so that you shall not be forced
To ask protection from him; he himself
Shall offer it, propose your flight, and aid
The whole proceeding. It shall be his plan.
You know how men will struggle for their own,
Even against justice. 'Tis a hopeful scheme.
Your cousin's time hangs dully on his hands;
He'll thank me for employment.

SOPHIA.

           Philip, Philip,
'Tis your old way; you always held your triumph
Before you won your victory.

KÖNIGSMARK.

           Hist! I see
A heavy shadow moving through the trees.
Some one approaches. Princess, it were well
If the conspirators were never seen
In secret conclave.

SOPHIA.

          I will leave you then.

Do not forget Duke Anthony. You men
Who start so wildly seldom reach your end
Unless by the first effort. Königsmark,
You are a greyhound, running by your sight;
One dash, and all is over; let the game
But gain a space upon your eager bounds,
And you have no nose to follow.

KÖNIGSMARK.
A while ago
You said I triumphed ere my victory;
I vow 'tis not your habit to reward
Before a service.

SOPHIA.
I am paid. Farewell!
[*Exit.*

KÖNIGSMARK.
Had I no fear my prayers would anger Heaven,
I'd call on Heaven to bless her. How dare I,
So stained with sin, so draggled and bemired
With the vile cleavings of my reckless course,
Insult her innocence with my foul love?
Her swinish husband's brutal appetite
But errs by instinct: I have given a mind
Stored with more riches than he ever knew
To the same service. In regard to her,
I am Prince George's better but in this,
That I am not her husband. Heavenly gifts
I have perverted to most earthly ends.
My heart, my intellect, my subtle eye,
That lays the mysteries of humanity
As bare to me as the dissector's knife
The body's secrets—that transcendent boon,

Imagination, by which poets talk
Full front with angels, and attain to heights
Of wondering knowledge, from which reason turns
Dizzy with weakness—these I have debased—
To what?—to mean ambition, avarice,
And the poor triumph of frail woman's tears.
I loathe my life. I know not where to hide
From the sharp glance of memory. Henceforth
The beast within my nature shall consume,
Die out amid its ashes. Hear me, Heaven!
I'll sin no more. Lo! even while I pray,
Temptation comes, and a despairing sense
Of unforgotten guilt, to close the gates
Of heaven against me.

(*Re-enter* COUNTESS VON PLATEN.)

COUNTESS VON PLATEN.

Ha! Count Königsmark!
Alone—no woman—not a sign of one!
You slight your old employment. Nay, look there!
Whose robe is that which flutters up the path?

KÖNIGSMARK.

I cannot tell.

COUNTESS VON PLATEN.

Or will not. Have you seen—
Pray look at me; you are discourteous, Count—
Have you not seen the Princess?

KÖNIGSMARK.

Seen what princess?

COUNTESS VON PLATEN.

Sophia Dorothea.

KÖNIGSMARK.

    Since when, madam?

COUNTESS VON PLATEN.

Since the creation. Pshaw! you answer me
With question upon question. Fear you me?
Philip, I am your friend.

KÖNIGSMARK.

    I am not yours;
You know it, madam. I am false as air;
And for that falsehood, where it fell on you,
You ought to hate me. Why, have you forgotten
The night you clung to me with desperate strength,
Sobbing and cursing, praying and commanding
That I would stay a moment; or at least
Utter one word of love before I went?
I wounded you in woman's tenderest spot;
I have not hoped to be forgiven.

COUNTESS VON PLATEN.

    You then
Have not forgotten?

KÖNIGSMARK.

    No.

COUNTESS VON PLATEN.

    Nor I. But, come,
Let us forget. I bear no malice now;
Besides, you are in danger.

KÖNIGSMARK.

    What of that?
Do you suppose I live my life without

Counting its dangers coolly? Any day
A jealous husband, or an outraged brother,
May call me to the field. I weighed this thing,
And practiced fencing.

    COUNTESS VON PLATEN.
      But your peril now
Is one you cannot master. Long success
Has made you over-confident. Your aim
Is too ambitious, dangerous to achieve,
And certain death to fail in. I believe
Sophia's temper colder than your heart;
Her virtue deeper than your wickedness;
Her duty more than your ingratitude;
And all her good so overbalancing
Even your ill, that failure is as sure
As after punishment.

    KÖNIGSMARK.
      Why, this is news!
Her station cuts me off from intercourse.
Had I the wish, the opportunity—
On which hang all things in affairs like this—
Is wanting. Bah! impossibilities
Are not the things I cope with. I must have
At least the common chances.

    COUNTESS VON PLATEN.
      Save your words
For simpler hearers. You should recollect
The dainty falsehoods you have helped me to,
And fear a surfeit, Count. I am your friend;—
Believe or not, the fact remains the same;—

And I would warn you—and inflame you, too,
Or I misjudge your nature. (*Aside.*)

    KÖNIGSMARK.

      Be at rest,
If your kind heart can find no other care.
Besides, my old pursuits begin to pall :—
You know my fickle character. I think
Of taking up religion, for the nonce,
By way of change. You know that the relapse
Will be—ah, so delicious!

    (*Enter* PRINCE GEORGE.)

    COUNTESS VON PLATEN.

     In good time—
Your Highness has come in quite à *propos.*
Here's a disciple for you, Königsmark. (*Aside to
 him.*)
What does your Highness think the Count designs?

    PRINCE GEORGE.
Heaven knows.

    COUNTESS VON PLATEN.
    To take religion up.

    PRINCE GEORGE.
     Ha! ha!

    COUNTESS VON PLATEN.
But for what purpose, think you?

    PRINCE GEORGE.
     I suppose
To ruin it.

COUNTESS VON PLATEN.

                No ; for the luxury
Of a relapse into his sins again

PRINCE GEORGE.

By Jove, that's rare !

COUNTESS VON PLATEN.

                But you must be devout,
You must outgo Saint Peter in your zeal,
Else you will not receive the fullest zest
From the relapse.

KÖNIGSMARK.

           I'll found a monastery.
My patron saint shall be—

COUNTESS VON PLATEN.

              Saint Anthony :
You know how he was tempted.

KÖNIGSMARK.

                You shall sit
Before the door, and be temptation. You
Shall be the world, the flesh, the devil, Countess,
All merged in one.

PRINCE GEORGE.

     O monstrous slanderer !

KÖNIGSMARK.

I wished to show how safe my house will be
With such a mild temptation.

COUNTESS VON PLATEN.

     Ah! my Count,
There'll be a bitter reckoning for this. (*Aside.*)

PRINCE GEORGE.

Where go you, now?

KÖNIGSMARK.

  To found my monkery.   [*Exit.*

PRINCE GEORGE.

You and Count Königsmark appear to be
Poor friends just now.

COUNTESS VON PLATEN.

     No, no; the very best,
Judging his latest manner. 'Tis his way:
He is a man who frowns upon his friends,
And fawns upon his foes. I ruffled him
By rating his presumption.

PRINCE GEORGE.

      About what?
He seems a harmless idler. Setting by
Some gallantries, in which his willing prey
Ran half the way to meet him, he may pass
As a good fellow in such days as these.

COUNTESS VON PLATEN.

He grows ambitious in his gallantries,
Deeming his victims types of our whole sex;
'Twas there I checked him.

PRINCE GEORGE.

   Pshaw! you sadden sport.
Let him aspire; what matter?

COUNTESS VON PLATEN.

        Duty, Prince,—
My duty to your father and his house
Is serious matter.

PRINCE GEORGE.

     Ha! would Königsmark
Play tricks with us? By Jove, the fellow's bold!
Who is the lady?

COUNTESS VON PLATEN.

     Has your Highness heard
The news from England? Things look promising
For Hanover. The Stuarts—

PRINCE GEORGE.

     Pray answer me.

COUNTESS VON PLATEN.

I beg your pardon. What did you inquire?

PRINCE GEORGE.

I ask for whom these amorous toils are set?

COUNTESS VON PLATEN.

What toils?

PRINCE GEORGE.

   Why Königsmark's, of whom we spoke.

COUNTESS VON PLATEN.

Ah! Königsmark?

PRINCE GEORGE.

    Zounds! yes. Do you forget
Your conversation as you utter it?

COUNTESS VON PLATEN.

No; but the news from England is so full
Of prosperous tidings—

PRINCE GEORGE.

      Hang your politics!
Keep them for the Elector. Answer me;
Who's the Count's lady-love?

COUNTESS VON PLATEN.

       I cannot say—
Or rather, please your Highness, dare not say.

PRINCE GEORGE.

Pish! you provoke me.

COUNTESS VON PLATEN.

      I would not provoke
Your Highness to inquire; because your peace
Is so concerned in this—

PRINCE GEORGE.

     How now! speak out!
You should have learned not to play hide and seek
With one of my rash temper.

COUNTESS VON PLATEN.

       If I speak,
I must disclose a truth—

PRINCE GEORGE.

     I hope so, madam.

KÖNIGSMARK.

COUNTESS VON PLATEN.

A truth—say a suspicion; for the truth
Remains to be established.

PRINCE GEORGE.

     Say a truth—
Say a suspicion—or, to please yourself,
Say a suspicion of a truth. 'Sdeath, Countess,
Say something! You bewilder me with words,
Suggesting, yet concealing, an affair
That, after all, may be a mere device
Tricked out by fraud or folly.

COUNTESS VON PLATEN.

    Does your Highness
Mistrust my truth?

PRINCE GEORGE.

    I shall mistrust your wits,
Or say you think but poorly of my own,
If this continue.

COUNTESS VON PLATEN.

    I would rather be
An open foe than a suspected friend.
Pray has your Highness not observed of late
That Königsmark and Princess—

PRINCE GEORGE.

    Ha! my wife!
That is your drift? 'Ods mercy! are you mad?
He and Sophia! Yes, yes, I have marked
Their talks and rambles. I have counted them
Brother and sister, as they think themselves.

Do you not know that, from their childish days,
They have been playmates?

COUNTESS VON PLATEN.

And may be again
Unless you mar their pastime. Playmates, too!—
Memories of childhood!—oh, what deadly stuff
For Königsmark to work with!

PRINCE GEORGE.

Have you grounds
For this suspicion?

COUNTESS VON PLATEN.

Common rumor, Prince,
The scandal of the Court, and my own eyes.

PRINCE GEORGE.

Have they been talked of?

COUNTESS VON PLATEN.

Talked of! They have worn
A hundred gossips' tongues out.

PRINCE GEORGE.

'Twere as well
To end their friendship.

COUNTESS VON PLATEN.

In its public show
I see no harm; but secret meetings, Prince,
Are full of danger.

PRINCE GEORGE.

Ha! but have they such?

COUNTESS VON PLATEN.

A while ago they parted on this spot,
Sophia flying as though winged by fear—
For what suppose you? but to shun my sight.
Prince, that looks ill.

PRINCE GEORGE.

    Looks ill! It looks like guilt.
Looks, Countess, mark me: you must not suppose
I think it guilt. Sophia is too cold—

COUNTESS VON PLATEN.

To you?

PRINCE GEORGE.

   To me, and all mankind.

COUNTESS VON PLATEN.

        Perhaps.—
Were I Count Königsmark, I'd pledge myself
To speak with certainty upon this point.

PRINCE GEORGE.

Fie! you would make me jealous.

COUNTESS VON PLATEN.

       I! in faith,
I would but turn you to your own affairs.
Do your own will: I shall not offer you
Even advice. If I have erred in this,
What harm is done? You have no heart to wound,
No sentimental suffering o'er your wrongs.
If it is true, I spoke in proper time;
And you should thank me, and bestir yourself.

C

PRINCE GEORGE.

You know what love I bear my Zellish wife;
I show it in my life. My father's plan
Was to wed Zell with Hanover; and there
He has succeeded, with but little care
For the poor pawns with which his move was made.
But she's my wife, my honor's in her hands,
And, by high heaven, she shall respect the pledge!
Were she not mine, Count Königsmark and she
Were welcome to their love. Ha! ha! by Jove,
All the Sophias in broad Hanover
May kiss his feet, but not my wife—my wife.
Were she an ape, a goat, a porcupine,
She should be sacred if she bore that name.
I'll see to this, and I expect your aid

COUNTESS VON PLATEN.

And so far as my duty—

PRINCE GEORGE.

               Poh! your duty!
You have some motives of your own I know,
But they are naught to me. If she prove false,
Zell may become the devil's heritage:
I swear, I will not, through a tainted wife,
Succeed to it, though the Elector rave
At my refusal. Countess, a good day! [*Exit.*

COUNTESS VON PLATEN.

Not jealous? You are bitten to the heart.
Storm at your wife, forbid her Königsmark,
And we shall have more secret interviews,
With keener relish for the stolen sweets.

If they are not in love, before a week
We'll drive them to it headlong. Jealousy,
Commend me to a thorough libertine
To learn thy nature. They who scorn our sex,
And make them playthings for their vanity,
Suffer at home, just grain for grain, the pangs
They spread abroad, suspicion poising sin.
I vow, my sense of justice gathers joy
From loose-lived George's ill-concealed distress.
When Philip Königsmark begins to writhe
In the great anguish of his coming fate,
I ask no heaven beyond the sight of it,
With power to tell him, in his misery,
I am the cause. Look in my flaming eyes,
And see a baleful prophecy of that
Which burns beyond the borders of this world—
That hell towards which you hasten,—and in which
I'll laugh for joy through all eternity,
Blessed as a saint, to see your sufferings! [*Exit.*

ACT II.

SCENE. *The State Apartment of the Palace. Figures cross the Stage, as if going to a Masquerade.* Enter the ELECTOR *and* COUNTESS VON PLATEN.

ELECTOR.

I'll not believe it. Never talk of proof.
This woman's stuff, this mawkish sentiment,
For ever creeps into affairs of state,
Laming our projects. Hearts! why, what have hearts
To do with policy? Sound government
Moves by inflexible machinery,
Crushing all interference with its laws.
I say Sophia is a part of this,
A train of wheels, and I'll not have her stopped
While she moves on so smoothly to my ends.
We judge a government by its results,
Not by its means. Zell and this girl are one;
And Hanover must swallow both, to be
The kingdom I intend her to become.

COUNTESS VON PLATEN.

But George is jealous.

ELECTOR.

Jealous! by what right?
Suppose Sophia shaped her life by his,
Paid him in kind for his inconstancy,
Why what a famous baggage she would be

With that rare pattern! She is far too good,
Too loyal and too patient for the rogue.
The contrast makes him darker than he is;
And, Heaven knows, that is needless. I could say
A thousand things in my defence of her,
Were she proved guilty without doubt; I scorn
To answer mere suspicion with a word.
Look at her face—

COUNTESS VON PLATEN.
    And Zell!

ELECTOR.
    Ay, look at Zell—
If you will reason on such grounds as these—
And I'll defend her were she Jezabel.

COUNTESS VON PLATEN.
Frankly said, Ernest! It is not my wish
To lose you Zell. Precaution, nothing more,
Is my advice. Maintain the character
Of your own family by timely care,
And all the threatened evils which you fear
May be avoided. You are fixed so high,
And look so far abroad, as to forget
The little people clustered at your feet.
Turn your eyes homeward.

ELECTOR.
    There is sense in that.
I'll end this matter at a single blow:
I'll banish Königsmark from Hanover.

COUNTESS VON PLATEN.
Before you know him guilty? Pray be just.

Your rashness is the sluggard's remedy
Against impending fears. Your government,
Conducted by such policy as this,
Would run your favorite shallop high and dry
Before a fortnight.

ELECTOR.

     Zounds! what shall I do?
You counsel action, yet oppose each act.

COUNTESS VON PLATEN.

I'll tell you what. We must begin at once
By strict investigation. We will know
What points we stand upon, what points we lack,
And to what truths these facts, when duly weighed,
Direct our judgment.

ELECTOR.

     Oh, yes; we shall know
All that we know, all that we do not know,
And to what ends our ignorance may tend.—
How wise we'll be! Elizabeth, my time
Is far too precious in its real results
To waste in busy idleness like this.
You, if you wish, may set your wits to work,
And chase these shadows for mere love of sport.
The chase alone must be your recompense.
I'll have no antlers hanging at my door,
No clarions heralding your victory,
Nothing to draw the notice of the world;
For, let me tell you, if you prove this girl
The devil's daughter, not the Duke of Zell's—
So the succession but remain in her—
I shall be deaf to all your arguments.

Now I commend you to your bootless task,
With my best wishes.   [*Exit.*

   COUNTESS VON PLATEN.
      I desire no more.
The match between Sophia and Prince George
Was my own plan. The fault of my device
Was that my puppet soon outgrew my hand.
But let me once destroy the hold she has
On the Elector, through her dowry—
O'erturn her influence, yet keep him Zell—
Kill his fair goose, yet get her golden egg;
And for the deed draw all his gathered wrath
On Philip Königsmark's devoted head—
And I shall be content. The course is plain,
Secure and rapid, yet I hesitate.
Why is this pause? An awful monitor
Whispers within me one prophetic word,
And it is blood, blood, blood! Oh, terrible!
I dare not trace my purpose to its end;
Yet I rush blindly on, as though my fate
Had snatched me in a hurricane from earth,
And hurled me forward. I will not shed blood.
What were the dreadful future to a soul
That in the face of apprehension looks
With my dismay! No; I will not shed blood—
Not even his.

   (*Enter* MADAM WREYKE.)

   MADAM WREYKE.
 Good heavens! what have you done?
George is as moody as a winter day;
Sophia keeps her chamber; Königsmark

Lowers suspiciously on all your friends;
And the Elector fidgets through the palace,
Searching our faces, with his asking eyes
Full of a question which he dares not breathe.

COUNTESS VON PLATEN.

These are but phases of the same disease,
Affecting different natures differently.
Prince George is jealous.

MADAM WREYKE.

     But too soon, I fear.
He was not ripe for jealousy.

COUNTESS VON PLATEN.

       Not ripe!
Why, when is jealousy not ripe? It springs,
Like Arctic moss, a strong and perfect plant
At the first flash of light. This jealousy
Has no degrees. 'Tis a most choleric
And nimble fiend. A sign, a look, a word
Has necromantic power to start it up
Blazing with wrathful questions. Listen, now:
Were there no obstacles between this pair
Of backward lovers, they might both grow gray
Unconscious of each other's passion. Place
A barrier between them, and you'll see
How they'll boil up to meet above the wall,
Or undermine it, or flow round about,
To mix their kindred currents as of old.
That obstacle is George's jealousy.
His mere suspicion may be first to teach
Sophia that she loves. Count Königsmark
Needs no preceptor.

MADAM WREYKE.

    Yes; but George's power
May interpose impossibilities.

COUNTESS VON PLATEN.

Impossibilities are Love's old playthings.
I'll trust to Love, and aid him at his need.
George's suspicion, too, prepares the way
For easy proof. And, by the by, have you
Aught of Sophia's? Say a fan, a glove,
A scarf, a ring, a jewel—anything
Known to be hers; some trifle, plainly marked
With her own cypher? George's jealousy
Is a devouring ogre, and craves food.
I am purveyor, and must find him meat,
Or, 'sdeath! I may be eaten in its place.

MADAM WREYKE.

No; I have nothing.

COUNTESS VON PLATEN.

     Get me something.

MADAM WREYKE.

       How?
And what shall I obtain?

COUNTESS VON PLATEN.

      What is the use
Of such a lover as your friend, Prince Max,
If not to get me—let me think—yes, yes!
If not to get me those fine Mechlin gloves
That all the women have been crazed about?

MADAM WREYKE.

What is your purpose with those Mechlin gloves?

COUNTESS VON PLATEN.

The less you know, the less will be your sin.
Get me the gloves.

MADAM WREYKE.

I'll try.

COUNTESS VON PLATEN.

Tell stupid Max
You wish to copy the embroidery,
And to return them secretly; for thus
The Princess will know nothing of the theft.
Warn him to keep your counsel.

MADAM WREYKE.

If he hear
The Princess slandered, with the gloves as proof,
I might as well warn a tornado, sister,
As bid him hold his peace. He'll blurt it out
In spite of me. He loves Sophia dearly,
And aches to serve her.

COUNTESS VON PLATEN.

He'll hear nothing.

MADAM WREYKE.

Well,
I'll set about it.

COUNTESS VON PLATEN.

See, he comes.

(*Enter* PRINCE MAX.)

PRINCE MAX.
   What, Countess,
Do you neglect the masquerade to-night?
Your interests suffer while you tarry here.
You should not leave so slippery a thing
As my good father's heart to guard itself.
As I came through, I saw a buxom mask
Toying with the Elector's hand.

COUNTESS VON PLATEN.
    Which hand?

PRINCE MAX.
Why, either; but I'll say it was the left—
Nearest the heart, and farthest from the right.

COUNTESS VON PLATEN.
Then I care not. The right hand is for me,
The one that holds the sceptre. Will you back
To be our escort?

PRINCE MAX.
   Pardon me; I wish
A word in private—

COUNTESS VON PLATEN.
   That will do; I'll go.
Where is Von Platen?

PRINCE MAX.
   Where was Menelaus
When Paris wooed his Helen?

COUNTESS VON PLATEN.

              Are you Paris?

PRINCE MAX.

Oh, no; his younger son.

COUNTESS VON PLATEN.

            Adieu? Your wit
Is disagreeable from antiquity:
I'll seek a fresher.

PRINCE MAX.

            Let me recommend
A wit that's fresher than the morning dew,
If one may trust opinion. Königsmark
Has made the dancers dance with merriment.
He shines alone there, like the mid-day sun:
The little stars, that show themselves sometimes,
Roll round him darkly. All the fairer side
Of our gay Court—maids, wives and widows—fight,
Like hungry tigresses, who shall be first
To throw herself beneath Count Philip's feet.
That ancient jest is fresh from Königsmark.
Von Platen came into the masquerade,
Accoutred as a warrior of old Greece,
When Königsmark saluted him, at once,
As "Menelaus," and the whole Court roared
Like a loose Bedlam. Poor Von Platen's vizard
Shriveled with blushes.

COUNTESS VON PLATEN.

        Villain! gross, gross villain! (*Aside.*)
Well, praised be heaven, that something makes them
    gay!

If we must stand as butts, I would not ask
A nobler archer than Count Königsmark
To shoot the shafts. The blunt and leaden heads
Of his bird-bolts make noise enough it seems;
But, ah, they do not pierce, as mine shall pierce,
When he is quarry, and I bend the bow. (*Aside.*)
[*Exit.*

PRINCE MAX.

See, where she sails, in full-blown womanhood,
One of my many mothers! Fairer she
Than all her predecessors. I grew proud
Of the Elector's taste in womankind
When I first saw your sister.

MADAM WREYKE.

Fie, you wretch!
You make more scandal than a tea-table.

PRINCE MAX.

How she must hate poor Königsmark!

MADAM WREYKE.

But why?

PRINCE MAX.

Because she praised him. To my simple mind,
There's something awful in a woman's praise.
'Tis like a bell chimed for a funeral;
The sweeter and the more prolonged its note,
The sadder the occasion. Tell me, dear,
When will your doughty husband be from home?

MADAM WREYKE.

He lives at home.

PRINCE MAX.

Why, so do most men.

MADAM WREYKE.

                                     Bah!
I mean by that, he seldom goes abroad.

PRINCE MAX.

Still, I suppose, he's peering at the moon
Through his huge telescope. Unhappy sage!
He must be jealous of the man in it.

MADAM WREYKE.

I fear that he is jealous of a man
Most strangely under the moon's influence.

PRINCE MAX.

Of me, you mean? I who am prudence, Kate,
Incarnate prudence, in these glaring days
When folly rides a horse, and daring vice
Bullies poor virtue in her very church.

MADAM WREYKE.

But you confound my husbands strangely, Max.
Poor Busché, my first victim, was the sage;
And he has not peeped through a telescope,
Nor opened a Greek grammar, since the day
Some waggish fellows bore him to his grave.
My old Endymion, for aught I know,
May now be in the moon he loved so well.

PRINCE MAX.

Then General Wreyké's looking after him
Through his own telescope.

MADAM WREYKE.

                Brave Wreyké is
A man of valor, a grim, bloody Mars,
Who cares no more for telescopes or Greek
Than I for him. Be careful how you talk.
You are always bringing the dead Busché up,
With warlike Wreyké's sabre in his hand;
Or making Wreyké bend his fiery eyes
To patient Busché's instruments.

PRINCE MAX.

                        In faith,
You taught me to confound them. Sage and soldier
Have equal life within my memory,
Where both are buried, with one wreath of love
Hung, as a votive garland, o'er their graves.
They were good people in their way, no doubt,
But of small moment, Kate, to you or me.
Let us not talk of them. Now answer me,
When shall I come?

MADAM WREYKE.

              To-morrow, if you choose,—
On one condition.

PRINCE MAX.

                One condition more!
When shall I reach my last condition, pray?

MADAM WREYKE.

When you are ill-conditioned, sick in bed,
Telling the priest whole histories of lies,
And, like the malefactor hung last week,
Fancy yourself a dying saint. But, Max,

'Tis not a hard condition. Bring to me
One of those Mechlin gloves the Princess wears,
Those famous gloves that we have all admired.
I wish to copy the embroidery
For a design that's private to myself,
And must not be divulged.

PRINCE MAX.

        An easy task.
I'll ask the Princess—

MADAM WREYKE.

      Nothing, if you please.
You'll steal it.

PRINCE MAX.

          Steal!

MADAM WREYKE.

     The Princess must not know
That I possess it. In a day or two,
I shall return the glove.

PRINCE MAX.

       But stealing gloves
Is not my line precisely. I am apt
At almost any kind of villainy;
But stealing, Kate, is something new to me;
I'll bungle at it. Then I may be whipped,
Put in the pillory, or Heaven knows what,
If I'm discovered.

MADAM WREYKE.

    . Will you bring the glove?

PRINCE MAX.
Yes.

MADAM WREYKE.
And in secret?

PRINCE MAX.
Yes.

MADAM WREYKE.
You'll never say
A word about it?

PRINCE MAX.
No, by—

MADAM WREYKE.
Do not swear:
I always doubt when you begin to swear.
I must return. The dancing is begun.

PRINCE MAX.
Then take my arm; and as we go along,
I pray you, blush a little for my sake.
My reputation as a libertine
Has been my making with your gentle sex.
Come, blush; and make them wonder what bad thing
I whisper to you.

MADAM WREYKE.
I shall blush perforce,
If you abuse humanity and sense
With such perverse and wicked calumnies.

PRINCE MAX.
Well, have it as you will. It seems to me,
The devil has been preaching here of late,

In father Bishop's empty pulpit-stand,
And to full benches, people run so mad.
Look there! why, bless me! here comes brother
    George
With his own wife!

MADAM WREYKE.
The world begins to mend.

PRINCE MAX.
Yes, certainly—on the outside, at least.
What will sweet George resort to after this?
He has exhausted Hanover, I think,
And needs must travel in pursuit of game.
He's now coquetting with the only woman
Whom he has not made love to in the Court.
What's to do after this venture?

MADAM WREYKE.
                Come along,
Oh! what a tongue to lay a wager on! [*Exeunt.*

(*Enter* PRINCE GEORGE, PRINCESS SOPHIA *and*
    COUNTESS VON KNESEBECK, *with Attendants,
    Pages, etc.*)

SOPHIA.
These are plain duties that belong to heaven,
And need no teaching. I have always tried
To shape my conduct to the public wish,
Living, in fear, a true slave to my state
Both as a wife and princess. If the world
Slanders my motives and suspects my acts,
The fault is in its own corrupted heart,
Not in my error. Philip Königsmark

Is my staunch friend, my earliest and best.
Wicked, you call him; I will not deny
The many gallantries you charge him with,
Nor ask indulgence for his lightest sin;
And yet, I say, the heart beneath all this
Is pure as nature so oppressed can be:
To me 'tis always pure. He comes to me,
Shaking the world's contagion from his robes,
Laying aside his years of wickedness,
His harmful thoughts, his schemes of future guilt,—
Ay, and, I hope, that gnawing misery
Which makes so hollow such a life as his,—
And stands before me but the simple boy
Who brought me early flowers and blossom-sprays,
When we were playmates in my home at Zell.

PRINCE GEORGE.

Grant it: I will not question aught of this;
I'll even blink Count Philip's character,
And swear that you and he are weaning lambs.—
Lambs for the slaughter you may be, ere long,
If you will graze together. If the world
Has scandalized you, though the charge be false,
Your damage is no less. There's but one thing
Which you must shun, and that is ill report.

SOPHIA.

Commands like these sound strangely from your mouth,
Whose conduct shouts defiance—

PRINCE GEORGE.

                Pray you, cease.
The sins I do, I carry; but your guilt

Is parted 'twixt us, and its stain descends
Upon your race.

SOPHIA.

My guilt!

PRINCE GEORGE.

Nay, understand;
I but suppose it for the argument.
I place no bar 'twixt you and Königsmark;
Your open friendship never will offend;
But I forbid your secret intercourse,
Your private meetings, your long *tête-à-têtes*,
Your looks of interchanged intelligence,
And all things else that may provoke the world
To censure your imprudence. This shall be!
And hark you, madam, where your duty fails,
Let your obedience help you.   [*Exit.*

COUNTESS VON KNESEBECK.

Princess, come.

SOPHIA.

Could ice be colder? Come! Where shall I go?
You see my husband has abandoned me
Upon the threshold of the Court. I feel
Like a poor wretch, upon whose poverty
The door is shut in fury. Shall I steal
Into the ball-room, at the Prince's heels,
Like an intruding cur? Oh! had I weeds,
Fit for a widow, with my widow's heart
I'd make a solemn entry. Here I stand,
A mark of wonder for my pitying train—
Insulted, scorned, deserted! Shall I turn

And crawl in sorrow to my slighted bed,
To wet its pillows with my fruitless tears?
Or shall I, in the majesty of my wrongs,
Enter the Court, with all the pomp I can,
And let this simple picture of my state
Appeal to men?

    COUNTESS VON KNESEBECK.
   Dear Princess, calm yourself;
You must grow used to this; your husband's heart
Is strange and wayward.

    SOPHIA.
    Heart! he has no heart—
No, nor that common worldly courtesy
With which men ape possession of a heart.
If fate has made me so unfortunate
As to be bound, unwillingly, to him,
Have I not grief enough, who know myself
Unloving and unloved, to satisfy
The slight annoyance which my presence gives?
I am no obstacle across his path;
He treads me underfoot. I stand aloof,
Holding his children back with either hand,
Meek, broken-hearted, abject; all I ask
Is decent pity, and some small regard
To that slight remnant of my wifely pride
Which is the right of woman. But his joy
Seems rather to consist in my distress
Than in the pleasure which his vices give.
Countess, I cannot bear it. To this point
I have struggled onward with my weary fate,
But here strength fails me. I must either die,
Or fling aside my burden.

(*Enter* KÖNIGSMARK.)

KÖNIGSMARK.
Princess.—

SOPHIA.
What brings you here? Philip!

KÖNIGSMARK.
Prince George's wish.

SOPHIA.
Indeed?

KÖNIGSMARK.
He ordered me to bring you to the masque.

SOPHIA.
He ordered you!

KÖNIGSMARK.
Yes; sent me a command
By Countess Platen. The first welcome word
That she has given to me for many a day.

SOPHIA.
But do you not distrust that woman?

KÖNIGSMARK.
Yes;
But such a heavenly message I'd have heard
From hell's ambassador.

SOPHIA.
Where is Prince George?

KÖNIGSMARK.

Trundling his little figure through the dance
With lofty Ermengarda. She is decked,
With flowers and gaudy bands, from head to heel;
So that her panting, dumpty lover looks
Much like a peasant dancing round a May-pole.

SOPHIA.

You do not mean—

KÖNIGSMARK.

   The murder's out at last.
She is acknowledged now to occupy
The very high but questionable post
Which rumor gave her. George has fitted up
A little palace for her; and to-morrow
She'll hold a court for all the villainy
That crawls to power by such unhallowed means.

SOPHIA.

This is too much!

KÖNIGSMARK.

   Not half enough, it seems;
Men wonder now what title and estate
Her gracious lord will lavish on her.

SOPHIA.

      Count!

KÖNIGSMARK.

Philip, not Count, dear Princess. Think of Zell.

SOPHIA.

You jeer at me.

KÖNIGSMARK.
                    At you!

SOPHIA.
              If not at me,
At my afflictions.

KÖNIGSMARK.
          If I give you pain,
First let me ask your pardon, and then Heaven's.
At infamy and outrage such as this,
A man must laugh or cry. I choose to laugh:
Weep you, poor sufferer; but remember this,—
Your heavy tears and my light merriment
Spring from one feeling. It is easier
To weep, as you do, than to laugh with me.

SOPHIA.
Now you are Philip once again. (*Removes her glove,
and extends her hand, which he kisses.*)

KÖNIGSMARK.
                    What eyes
Are those which glimmer through the corridor?
The Countess Platen!

SOPHIA.
                    She!

KÖNIGSMARK.
          Ay; look you there,
How she is gliding rapidly away;
And now your husband joins her at the door.
They enter, talking eagerly.

SOPHIA.
Of what?

KÖNIGSMARK.
Of you, of me, of mischief. Lies, lies, lies,
Past my imagination. Now, Prince George,
If you have sense within your earthy mind,
Let it bestead you; for the wily snake
That tempted Eve is whispering in your ear
Counsel as damning.

SOPHIA.
Philip, we are snared.

KÖNIGSMARK.
I see the trap. If we betray ourselves,
We cannot rail at the deceiver's craft.

SOPHIA.
What is her purpose?

KÖNIGSMARK.
To enrage Prince George
With jealous fancies of yourself and me.
Suspicion is a monster that grows fat
By food which reason starves on. Let us be
As wary as her ladyship is false.
Dear Princess, if the sun went out in heaven—
If planets, moon and stars were shrunk to naught
In the thick blackness, and the torpid earth
Groped blindly onward in her useless flight—
Poor nature's children would pray death to strike,
Perhaps usurp his rights. So I, aghast
At the dread mandate which must be pronounced,

Sicken, in selfish terror, of a doom
That seems eternal darkness unto me.—
We must not meet again.

SOPHIA.

    Philip, you rave.
What desperation would you urge me to,
By this cruel threat? My husband has forbidden
Our private meetings, as he calls the walks
Which we have taken through the palace grounds;
But even he had not your hardihood;
He would not tear me from you altogether.
He did not cavil at such friendly acts
As may be done in public.

KÖNIGSMARK.

    Gracious Heaven!
There is no spark of love within her heart!
Friendship is all—no more;—her candor proves it.
  (*Aside.*)
You guess my meaning. I shall not transcend
Your husband's orders, Princess. I ne'er wished
To draw a scandal on your spotless life,
By shunning you in public. Such a course
Would ask suspicion to make free with you.

SOPHIA.

You will not fly me then?

KÖNIGSMARK.

    No; I ne'er thought
Of such a thing. But have you no regret
For what our childhood has bequeathed to us,—
That sweet communion which blessed my life,

And kept a corner sacred in my heart,
Around whose magic circle all the fiends
Clamored in vain? I am bereft indeed.
I had a hope of heaven, still bright for me,
Within that starry centre of my soul.
The hope is fled: I turn my eyes within,
And all is darkness.

SOPHIA.
    Yes; but—

KÖNIGSMARK.
     Oh, enough!
Why should I murmur, if you seem content?
To-morrow evening, if there be no check,
I'll see Duke Anthony, and plead your cause.
A little interval of worldly care
May pass between that meeting and your flight,
And then we part for ever.

SOPHIA.
    Philip, nay—

KÖNIGSMARK.
For heaven's sake, peace! or I shall rave outright!
Why stand we here, while spies and enemies
Interpret our behavior as they wish?
Come to the masque. If fate have more in store,
I'll meet her anger with a mocking laugh.
I have lost all: why should I care to set
My worthless life against the smallest stake?
Come; they shall see how dear a thing it is
To play at ventures with a desperate man!

SOPHIA.

I do not understand you.

KÖNIGSMARK.

                That is well;
Faith is above all knowledge.

SOPHIA.

                I have that.
(*As they exeunt, she drops her glove.*)

(*Re-enter* PRINCE MAX *and* MADAM WREYKE.)

PRINCE MAX.

Sweetheart, you leave us early.

MADAM WREYKE.

                I am tired.

PRINCE MAX.

Why so am I; but my fatigue will last;
I shall not 'scape it with a little sleep.
Ah me! what labor, what consuming care,
Heart-burning, bitterness, spite, envy, hate,
Besotted luxury, qualms and regrets,
Are bound up in that false and vacant word
Which men call pleasure! Pleasure, what is it?
Simply anticipation. What is pain?
A retrospect of what we meant for joy.
Life is inverted to the backward glance;
And like a faulty picture, which we turn
Towards a clear mirror, doubles its defects
By the reflection. Poh! I'll hang myself,
If I proceed with fancies such as these.

There is but one receipt against our woes—
A painful process—heat and chill the heart
Until you make it steel.

MADAM WREYKE.
     Are you engaged
In this rare business?

PRINCE MAX.
    I have little need;
Others will do it for me.—Ha! look, Kate!
Here is the glove we sought for. (*Picks it up.*)

MADAM WREYKE.
      That is it.
How fortunate!

PRINCE MAX.
    To us; but for Sophia,
Who owns and lost the glove, I cannot say—
"How fortunate!" What a one-sided view
You women take of fortune! and that view
Always your own, counting no other's cost.

MADAM WREYKE.
What a fine moralist you grow! But, come,
Conduct me to my carriage. Bear in mind,
You are to keep the secret of this glove.

PRINCE MAX.
Trust me.

MADAM WREYKE.
  I must. I'll wager you a crown,
That you'll betray me ere the week be out.

PRINCE MAX.

Done, for a thousand!

(*Re-enter* COUNTESS VON KNESEBECK.)

COUNTESS VON KNESEBECK.

Has your Highness seen
A glove of Mechlin lace upon the floor?

PRINCE MAX.

Why, what is Mechlin lace? Some cobweb thing,
That blew out at the window, I suppose.
You women go in such a flimsy garb
That I oft wonder how you hold together.

COUNTESS VON KNESEBECK.

'Tis a lace glove, of priceless rarity,
Much valued by the Princess.

PRINCE MAX.

Tell your mistress,
She should not set her heart on such light things.
I'll send my Bishop father to her room,
To rate her on her vanity. As he
Will be his own example of the sin,
'Twill be light labor.

COUNTESS VON KNESEBECK.

Madam, pray explain
The matter to his Highness. You may chance
To light upon the glove—for here 'twas lost—
And do the Princess service.

MADAM WREYKE.

Certainly.

The Princess knows my love for her too well
To doubt my service.

    PRINCE MAX.
    O kind Heaven, be deaf!
Here comes a lie, a thorough female lie—
Downright and simple—without if or but—
To dare thy judgment! (*Aside.*)

    MADAM WREYKE.
    We came hither, Countess,
Just as the Princess left—

    PRINCE MAX.
      And if the glove
Had been upon the floor, undoubtedly
We should have seen it. Let me save her soul,
At my own peril. (*Aside.*)

    COUNTESS VON KNESEBECK.
     Probably, the glove,
By its own beauty, made some knave a thief.

    PRINCE MAX.
Yes, probably. There's but one step between
Sin and temptation. When the devil baits
His big hooks, Countess, the leviathans
Bite like mere gudgeons.
    [*Exit* COUNTESS VON KNESEBECK.
    Oh! oh! Katharine,
Could you but see your face!

    MADAM WREYKE.
      I wonder not;
I am blushing for your falsehood.

PRINCE MAX.

     In your cause.
A miracle has saved me from a theft.
I should thank Heaven that sent the smaller sin,
And swallow it in silence. But I lied—
I lied most roundly—did I not, sweet Kate?

MADAM WREYKE.

Most roundly, Max, and with such natural grace!
You've found your calling.

PRINCE MAX.

    But I did not steal:
And there's no law for liars.

MADAM WREYKE.

     Or you'd hang.

PRINCE MAX.

Now, after all, what is the glove to you?
Your purpose with it is an idle whim;
Let me restore it.

MADAM WREYKE.

     In a day or two.

PRINCE MAX.

I vow, it hangs upon my conscience, Kate;
I shall not rest until I take it back.—
Oh! curse the glove!

MADAM WREYKE.

    Order my carriage round.
I'll join you shortly in the vestibule.
Lay by your gloom.

PRINCE MAX.
   To lie and steal with grace!
These are two pretty steps 'twixt youth and manhood!
I feel as I were entering upon life
Through the gaol-door.

MADAM WREYKE.
     Be careful, or perhaps
You'll exit through it.

PRINCE MAX.
     What a comforter
Was lost to Job by your belated birth!   [*Exit.*

MADAM WREYKE.
I wonder what Elizabeth will do
    (*Re-enter* COUNTESS VON PLATEN)
With this same glove? It seems a trifling tool,
To be employed in her large business.

COUNTESS VON PLATEN.
 (*Taking the glove.*)   Hark!
Once on a time, I saw an engineer,
With hammer, chisel and some sooty stuff,
At work upon the huge foundation stones
Of a great rock. I paused, half merrily,
To wonder what the silly fellow meant
By his mean labor with so vast a thing.
Anon, there came a crash; the frightened earth
Shook under me; light failed; the startled air
Buffeted round me like an angry sea:
I almost swooned for terror. When I looked,

There stood the engineer; but at his feet
Lay the great rock, a ruin.   Even thus,
When Hanover is shaken by this glove,
You'll rather wonder at the grand effect
Than at the trifling instrument.   Adieu!
                              [*Exeunt severally.*

ACT III.

SCENE. *The Garden of the Palace.* *Enter* KÖNIGSMARK.

KÖNIGSMARK.

I have traced them one by one, the winding paths
Our loitering footsteps have so often trod.
How lonely seems yon walk which strays between
The lilac border and the boxwood hedge,
Though every tree hangs its pale violet blooms,
In drooping clusters, to the thievish air
That steals the perfume, and, with ingrate haste,
Forsakes its benefactor! There the path
Swerves from the sun, and plunging in the grove,
Is lost in dubious shadows. I, who stand
Under the frown of fortune, should consign
My sullen spirit to yon lowering wood:
This fair scene mocks me. Painted and unreal
Seems every flower; the swaying trees no more
Wave gentle invitations to repose;
Sternly they shake their threatening arms at me,
And whisper to themselves a tale of woe
Shaped from my future. Far above my head
The hard and steely sky encloses me
In its wide vault; and the o'erbrooding sun,
Like the high cresset in a felon's cell,
Glares in my face with its unwinking eye
Ablaze with coming vengeance. Gracious Heaven!
I merit it. 'Tis bitter, but 'tis just,
That Nature should forsake the erring man,

Now in his need, who in prosperity
Abused her bounty.   Shall we never meet—
Never again?   Must the last glimpse of light
Go out before me, as I stagger on,
Through the lone darkness, to my darker end?
The shadow on my way is from myself,
Turning my back against the blessed sun.
Sin and remorse have wrapped my life in gloom;
But, like a shipwrecked sailor without chart
Or guiding needle, I preferred the night
And its fair star, by which my course was steered,
To aimless daylight. . Yes, this love of mine
Itself is sin—a sin that looks like virtue
Against the darker background of my crimes;
But yet a sin, an insult to her truth,
And a wide blot upon my sullied soul
Before eternal eyes.
     (*Enter* COUNTESS VON PLATEN)
    There is no gate,
So wide and lofty, in the walls of heaven,
As to admit the burden which I bear:
I cannot shake it off: hell yawns—

   COUNTESS VON PLATEN.
      Yes, Count;
Hell yawns, and all the devils yawn with it,
To hear so ripe a sinner uttering
Such green morality.

   KÖNIGSMARK.
  What brought you here?

   COUNTESS VON PLATEN.
The season tempted me.   These early flowers

Blew their sweet breath across my window-sill,
And so I came. But I would not intrude,
If you are waiting for some fairer flower—
A pure white lily, modest violet,
Or, better still, a passionate young rose—
A princess, all aglow with life and fire,
Carnation to the centre. As for me,
I am a homely plant, a kitchen-herb,
And dare not claim your notice. I'm for use ;—
You found me useful once, to spice your dish,
When banqueting was rarer.

KÖNIGSMARK.

       Wait, and see
What flower will bloom. In penetrating power
You overpeer your odorous sisterhood.
The kitchen-herb is sage.

COUNTESS VON PLATEN.

       Why, true,
Sage is a kitchen-herb.

KÖNIGSMARK.
You help my wit.

COUNTESS VON PLATEN.
When your wit halts.

KÖNIGSMARK.
It bears me limping off. (*Going.*)

COUNTESS VON PLATEN.
Stay, Count, a word. Our—what shall I call it?—
 love?

KÖNIGSMARK.

Yes; call it love. Love is a hardy boy,
And carries more things than belong to him.
Poor Love is Passion's porter.

COUNTESS VON PLATEN.

Very well:
We'll call the feeling that arose between
Your heart and mine—for want of truer name—
Love, simply love.

KÖNIGSMARK.

For want of truer name.

COUNTESS VON PLATEN.

Your protest was included with my own;
But, if it ease your conscience, enter it
Once more. Or, if you wish it, every time
That I say " love," you'd better add to it
" For want of truer name." Well, Count, this love
Has reached the Elector's ears; and he—smile on—
Is jealous, as old men are apt to be
Who balance merits with a man like you.—
Good Heaven, Count Philip! here the Elector comes,
And with Von Platen too!

KÖNIGSMARK.

Where, Countess, where?

COUNTESS VON PLATEN.

There, through the linden-walk.

KÖNIGSMARK.

Is that the Elector?

COUNTESS VON PLATEN.
Doubtless; and I know Von Platen by his stoop.

KÖNIGSMARK.
You gave him that. A skillful artisan
Knows his own work.

COUNTESS VON PLATEN.
Count, would you ruin me?

KÖNIGSMARK.
How, Countess?

COUNTESS VON PLATEN.
By your loitering.

KÖNIGSMARK.
Run away,
If you are frightened. As for me, in sooth,
I feel no terror of that ancient pair.

COUNTESS VON PLATEN.
But were we seen together?

KÖNIGSMARK.
If you flee,
We'll not be seen together.

COUNTESS VON PLATEN.
But were you
Found standing here, and the least glimpse of me
Caught, as I fled?—

KÖNIGSMARK.
What then?

COUNTESS VON PLATEN.

It would confirm
The Elector's worst suspicion. Königsmark,
You dally cruelly with the fate of one
Who gave you all. Prize or despise the gift,
It was my best, and offered for your sake.
A vestal's love, in her own eyes, could be
No more than the insulted, humbled heart
Which I bestowed upon you : 'twas my all.
Nay, then, we'll fall together. Here I'll stand,
Close by your fortunes, and divide the worst.
When this disgraceful scandal steals abroad,
Some, whose respect you hold in high esteem,
Will wonder at you—but with less respect.

KÖNIGSMARK.

True. (*Aside.*)

COUNTESS VON PLATEN.

See, they come directly towards this spot.

KÖNIGSMARK.

Madam, command me.

COUNTESS VON PLATEN.

Victory! (*Aside.*) This way.
(*As they exeunt, she drops* SOPHIA's *glove.*)

(*Enter* PRINCE GEORGE *and* COUNT VON PLATEN.)

PRINCE GEORGE.

This is a rendezvous. We have disturbed
A pair of billing doves. See, see, Von Platen,
How they go fluttering through the trees!

VON PLATEN.

       Ha! ha!
The man is surely Königsmark. Pray, note
His stately stride behind his lady-love.

PRINCE GEORGE.

Yes; it is Königsmark. His dignity
Is no companion for his lady's fright.
I wish we'd caught them. Love has nimble eyes
For coming danger. 'Tis a pretty spot
For dalliance truly. Mark yon laurel bower,
Walled in with leaves, yet full of loop-holes, too,
And the thick hedge that circles it around:
This is Love's citadel. And here are posies—
Roses in every shape, from bud to flower,
Violets, lilies, heartsease, spicy pinks—
To say sweet things about, and furnish love
With dainty figures for his rhetoric.
'Sdeath, Count, I wonder who the lady—
    (*Picks up* SOPHIA's *glove.*)

VON PLATEN.

       Ha!
Have you found proofs? Good Heaven, your Highness, why—
Why do you glare upon that glove? Nay, Prince,
Is it a goblin?

PRINCE GEORGE.

    No; 'tis but too real.
Von Platen, read that cypher.

VON PLATEN.

       Wonderful!

PRINCE GEORGE.
Vile, damnable!

VON PLATEN.
Your Highness does not think—

PRINCE GEORGE.
Think, man! I know. I do not wish to see
The thing I loathe to think on. Guilty wives
Play not their capers in the market-place:
Oh no; they come to bowers, to spots like this,
Filled with their wicked cunning, and disgrace
Fair nature and themselves at once.

VON PLATEN.
      But, Prince,
The glove by chance—

PRINCE GEORGE.
      The glove by fate, I say!—
'Twas fate alone that plucked it from her hand,
And left it here before my outraged eyes.
Wall guilt about with solid adamant,
And it will murmur on till some one hear;
Sink it beneath the waves, and it will rise
At the first thunder; bury it in earth,
And, at fit season, it will sprout and bear
Its bitter fruitage. Guilt, like the deaf man
That whispers to himself unconsciously,
Knows not that others hear. Against its will,
It is its own advertisement.

VON PLATEN.
      Your Highness
May wrong your wife by hasty judgment.

PRINCE GEORGE.
                    Ah!
If it were news, I could be merciful,
And doubt my own conclusions. But this thing
Has been the tattle of the Court for months:
Your wife has heard it,—nay, herself has seen
Such private meetings, in secluded nooks,
As this which we have interrupted. More,
But yesterday I charged my wife to hold
No further interviews with Königsmark;
She cunningly assented to my wish;
And here you have the fresh, unbroken fruit
Of her obedience. She does not take time
Even to forget my wishes, but sails on
Serenely towards her port, as though my breath
Were morning vapor.

VON PLATEN.
                Surely you'll not charge
The Princess with a crime.

PRINCE GEORGE.
                I make no charge:
I am in the dark with you. But what's to do
With disobedience, if it run at large?
She has discovered what a precious thing
The Elector holds her and her Zell to be;
And thus supported, with audacious front,
She sinks my fame beneath her dirty lands,
And dares me to the issue. What am I,
Against a wife and father such as these?
I tell you, I am helpless. Let her step
One foot into the daylight, show one sign
Of certain guilt, and were she lineal heir

To the broad earth, I'd take a husband's rights
With her transgression!

VON PLATEN.

     Patience, patience, Prince!
Doubts and suspicions are not evidence.

PRINCE GEORGE.

I prove no more than what her conduct shows.
I'll call her disobedient, nothing else;
And yet I think her hasty flight, just now,
Argues her damned, in her own eyes at least,
And gives us color for a like belief
Count Königsmark shall answer—

VON PLATEN.

       Answer what?
Will you proclaim your own dishonor, Prince,
On a suspicion?

PRINCE GEORGE.

     Your advice is wise.
I shall be patient to a certain point;
But after that, you'll find me deaf as death
To timid counsel, pity, or respect.
Zounds! Count, look yonder! Here Sophia comes!
For what, I pray you? Is the woman mad,
To seek my anger?
 (*Enter* SOPHIA *and* COUNTESS VON KNESEBECK.)
      How now, madam, still
At your old haunts! Our talk of yesterday
Rests lightly on your memory.

SOPHIA.

                           Not so;
No syllable has faded yet. Some words
Impress themselves upon the hardest heart,
By greater hardness. I have brought my friend,
The Countess Knesebeck, as body-guard
Against gallants.

PRINCE GEORGE.

     Your wit is sprightly.

SOPHIA.

                              Yes;
Your jealous humors form so wide a butt,
That the most simple wit may strike, by chance,
An outer ring.

PRINCE GEORGE.

     Von Platen, this is cool. (*Aside to him.*)
May I inquire what purpose brought you here?

SOPHIA.

Two purposes: the need of exercise,
And the slight hope of finding, in my walk,
A glove of Mechlin lace which I have lost.

PRINCE GEORGE.

Ah, ha! Mark that. (*Aside to* VON PLATEN.) Is
   this the glove?

SOPHIA.

                           Yes, yes!
Oh! thank your Highness! You must not suppose
I hold this trifle higher than its worth.

I had a woman's fancy for these gloves,
Because no woman has the match to them.
At such a reason, you, as men, may laugh,
But 'twere deep logic to a female court.

PRINCE GEORGE.

How came it here?

SOPHIA.

    Why, that is strange indeed.
I thought I wore it to the masquerade.
The Countess saw it on my hand too.

COUNTESS VON KNESEBECK.

        Yes;
As we were entering the ante-room.

PRINCE GEORGE.

Here is fine acting! Did you ever hear
Lies overloaded so with circumstance?
They must have practiced at a looking-glass,
Before they sallied forth to try their art
On our credulity. (*Aside to* VON PLATEN.)

SOPHIA.

     Perhaps the glove
Was stolen; or found, and lost again.

COUNTESS VON KNESEBECK.

       Perhaps
The robber feared detection, having heard
What stir you made about it.

PRINCE GEORGE.

     Blessed saints!

What eagerness these women have to lie!
They catch the falsehood from each other's mouth,
For fear of being outstripped. (*Aside to* VON
 PLATEN.)

SOPHIA.
   But tell me, Prince,
Where was it found?

PRINCE GEORGE.
   Here.

SOPHIA.
   Here! Who found it?

PRINCE GEORGE.
    I.

COUNTESS VON KNESEBECK.
That is a strange—

PRINCE GEORGE.
   You reckless sinner, cease!
Think me, and make me, whatsoe'er you will;
I will not be called wittol to my teeth.

SOPHIA.
Your Highness—

PRINCE GEORGE.
   Shameless trickster, dare you play
Such wretched antics in the open air,
With nothing 'twixt you and the thunderbolt,
That lightly slumbers in yon murky cloud,
But heavenly mercy?

SOPHIA.

Is your Highness sane?

PRINCE GEORGE.

Dare you deny the evidence of sense?

SOPHIA.

Yes, if God's truth oppose it.

PRINCE GEORGE.

Impudent!
Would you outface us with transparent lies,—
Set up your mere denial, to persuade
Von Platen and myself, that what we saw,
We saw not?

SOPHIA.

Pray, what saw you?

PRINCE GEORGE.

Ah!
You'll not commit yourself, until you know
The utmost limit of the adverse charge;
You will not give the slightest vantage-ground,
By one incautious word. Does this appear
Like truth, like innocence? No, no; it shows
The tricky sharpness of the advocate.

SOPHIA.

And is it contrary to human law,
That the accused, in such a cause as this,
Defend herself? I have no advocate,
Save my own wit, against an unknown charge.
This is wild justice. You yourself assume
The judge's ermine and the accuser's gown;

Prejudge my cause, pass sentence without trial;
Denying me the common right of speech,
Even on the scaffold.

PRINCE GEORGE.

     This shall not avail.
You saw, Von Platen; you shall question her.
I'll lay aside a husband's rights and powers,
Letting my judgment stand a listener.
'Sdeath! do you think me hasty of belief
'Gainst my own honor?

SOPHIA.

    'Gainst your honor, Prince!
I am your honor's guardian: I alone
Support that fiction to a doubting world.
You have done all that reckless hands could do
To blot the patent which you held from heaven;
And now you turn, with prodigal excess,
To pluck the remnant which I hold in trust—
Ah! not for you, you spendthrift of all worth,
But for our children. Let me render them
A name unsullied, on one side at least,
As their poor portion.

PRINCE GEORGE.

     Hear her, Heaven!

SOPHIA.

      Ay, hear!
If thou dost ever bend thy open ear
To bad men's supplications, hark to this;
And let his angry words arise, transformed
To something holy by a mother's prayer!

PRINCE GEORGE.

Bold hypocrite! Von Platen, to your work!

VON PLATEN.

I pray your Highness—

PRINCE GEORGE.

I will have it so.

VON PLATEN.

Am I commanded?

PRINCE GEORGE.

On your loyalty.

VON PLATEN.

Believe me, Princess, 'tis a loathful task.

SOPHIA.

I shall believe you as I find you, sir;—
But be not backward.

VON PLATEN.

These then are the facts:
His Highness and myself came walking hither,
Absorbed in conversation. As we turned
From yonder linden-alley towards this bower,
We saw two figures stealing from our sight,
As if to shun us. One was Königsmark;
We knew him by the boldness of his gait
And by his lordly person. She who ran
Before the Count, bending her body down,
As if to screen herself by her companion,
We could not recognize. I'll say no more;
But here we found your glove.

PRINCE GEORGE.

    Dry, almost warm—
, trace of dew upon a thread of it;—
And yet 'tis early morning. I'll be sworn,
That glove lay not upon the watery grass
Since yester-eve—no, not one hour.

SOPHIA.
       I think
The lady dropped it.

PRINCE GEORGE.
    What?

SOPHIA.
    And yet, I say,
That lady was not I.

PRINCE GEORGE.
    Oh! marvelous!

COUNTESS VON KNESEBECK.

How so, your Highness? What the Princess lost,
Another one may find, and lose again.

PRINCE GEORGE.

I'll credit anything—put faith in dreams,
In conjurors, in wantons—ere I shake
In this conviction.

SOPHIA.
   ·But are you quite sure
The man was Königsmark?

VON PLATEN.
Of that one fact
There is no doubt.

SOPHIA.
I'm sorry.

PRINCE GEORGE.
Keep your grief
For your own use. This feignéd innocence—
I'll not deny you have the trick of it,
To rival nature—does not hoodwink me.

SOPHIA.
Your Highness doubts me!

PRINCE GEORGE.
Doubt you! should I not?
Would one, corrupt in everything besides,
Shrink from or stammer at a spoken lie?

SOPHIA.
Gross man, the indignation which I feel
Should find a tongue; but I will calm myself
Down to the level of a patient wife.
I know my duty; and I further know
The scoff and spurn of the whole universe
Can never make me other than I am,
As spotless as the heaven that wraps me round.
Hear me, Prince George! I'll put my pride to sleep,
And answer you straightforward to the point:
As Heaven's my witness, I have nowhere seen
Count Königsmark to-day!

COUNTESS VON KNESEBECK.
     And let me join
My lady's full avowal with my voice.
Since she arose I have not left her side;
And, as I hope for mercy on my sins,
Her words are solemn truth!

VON PLATEN.
     Where were you then
A half hour since, and in whose company?
Your whereabout is capable of proof,
I doubt not, Princess.

SOPHIA.
     Silence, insolent!
Your Countship is mistaken; it would seem,
From questions such as these, that you suppose
You are inquiring of the character
Borne by your own pure, excellent, dear wife.
'Twere unbecoming to my station, Count,
To bandy questions and replies with you.
I shall remember I'm of princely rank;
Forget not your condition. If the Prince
Would humble me with questions, let him ask;
I shall reply as meekly as I can.
You heard my broad assertion of my truth,
And I repeat it to you. Do you think
That your good wife would venture such an oath,
Were you to try her?

PRINCE GEORGE.
     Madam, you are pert.
Answer the question.

SOPHIA.

      Half an hour ago
I was shut up within the nursery,
At play among my children. There, indeed,
I am secluded. No one comes to them,
Save those whose duties bring them sourly in—
Not even their father.

PRINCE GEORGE.

    After that?

SOPHIA.

       I sewed
Upon a sampler, in my private room.—
Mark, where I pricked my finger, Prince.

PRINCE GEORGE.

    What next?

SOPHIA.

My robe was changed, my walking-shoes put on,—
Ay, and my hair was dressed. Pray, bend your
  head,
And you may scent the fresh pomatum.

PRINCE GEORGE.

      Then?

SOPHIA.

I put my mantle round me, drew my hood
Over my forehead, to avoid the sun,
And by so many steps as I can stride
Between this place and yonder palace-door,
Came here right onward. By the way I coughed,

Hemmed twice or thrice, and plucked a flower or
    two—
Here are the flowers; and then—

> PRINCE GEORGE.
>
> You jest with us.

> SOPHIA.

Where could a jest come in with better grace?

> PRINCE GEORGE.

Then you have not seen Königsmark?

> SOPHIA.
>
>   You heard
My solemn oath to that, twice registered,
For your conviction; and you also heard,
If you had doubts, the needless perjury
With which the Countess followed up my words.
I have spoken truly, as a lady may;
If you would have me answer as a felon,
You must arraign me in another court.

> PRINCE GEORGE.

Your story seems like truth.

> SOPHIA.
>
>   Seems, only seems!
Naught but defect of mind can make it false.
Go to the nursery, call in my maids,
Torture my helpless children till they speak,
Stretch my French hair-dresser upon the rack,
Propose some awful and tremendous form
Of affirmation to the Countess here,

Build up a stake and faggots for your wife,
If you would push this business to an end:
Only deal not with Philip Königsmark,
In your grand inquisition, if you're wise;
For, let me say, his proud soul would not speak
Upon compulsion, if the deviltry
Of all the Holy Office held itself
Obedient to your nod.

    PRINCE GEORGE.
      Your eloquence
Grows great again upon your favorite theme.
Your foolish and intemperate admiration
Betrays in spirit what it lacks in fact.
Give you and him the devil's golden gift,
Bare opportunity, and I will back
Temptation against virtue, ten to one.

    SOPHIA.
Wanton insulter! would you drive me on
To desperation? Would you make me false?
Oh! were not virtue centred in herself,
Both law and solace to the tempted heart—
Dwelling, like God, amid her own pure light,
And needing nothing more beyond herself—
Self-nurtured, self-rewarded, self-sustained—
Heaven knows what fancies outrage and revenge
Might have begotten in my troubled soul
Long, long ere this! I pray you, pause a while :·
I am but human, and my misery
May mount above control.

    PRINCE GEORGE.
      Fine verbiage this!

SOPHIA.

In Heaven's name, leave me, Prince!

PRINCE GEORGE.

     I shall, unasked.
My stay belies my wish, and flatters you.
When you are strolling in this place again,
Be careful of your gloves. Von Platen, come!
     [*Exit with* VON PLATEN.

SOPHIA.

I am resolved. This is not want of love,.
Such as indifference may calmly bear,
Nor mere disgust, nor common tyranny,—
'Tis gross, malignant hatred.

COUNTESS VON KNESEBECK.

     Such as fiends
May feel for angels, better than themselves—
A hungry, thirsty and insatiate hate
That gnaws itself, unless its victim's blood
Redden its ruthless fangs. I'll say no more:
Throw prudence to the wind, and act your will.
I'd rather flee for refuge to the wolves,
Than live in splendor so unhappily.
Fly to Duke Anthony. I'll aid your plans,
And share your flight.

SOPHIA.

    My tried and steadfast friend,
You still forget the care you owe yourself,
In your regard for me. Count Königsmark
Designs a visit to Duke Anthony
This very night, returning ere the dawn,

If speed may compass it. I have no fear
Touching the answer that will come to me.
Duke Anthony would peril all his worth,
To do the house of Hanover some turn
To set it groaning. I shall rest secure
In his protection; for he'd wear his sword,
Down to the hilt, in his defence of me,
So that our enemies may only be
The best of Hanover. Ah, faithful heart,
Your eyes are glittering with joyful tears
At thought of my escape.

COUNTESS VON KNESEBECK.

Not only that;
The safe asylum, the untroubled rest,
After these storms have blown their fury out,
Would draw this tribute from less loving eyes
That look upon your fortunes.

(*Re-enter* KÖNIGSMARK, *behind.*)

SOPHIA.

Nay, you wrong
Your deep affection, by supposing it
A wide and common feeling. Hanover
Is broad and populous, my heart is soft,
And open, as the flowers before the sun,
To warming friendship; yet I still must say
That, when I came here, I brought all my friends:
I have found none, not one, for all my need.
You and—

KÖNIGSMARK.

And Philip Königsmark, you'll say,
If you deal fairly with that humble man.

SOPHIA.

What, after all your warnings given to me,
About our dangerous meetings, are you first
To break your resolution? Königsmark,
There's a pervading weakness in your mind
That, some time, will undo you. Look to that.

KÖNIGSMARK.

There's a pervading weakness in my heart
That strengthens me in action, and preserves
The little good my sinful nature holds.
Of that I am proud. I stood, observing you,
As exiled Adam by his garden's gate,
Gazing in grief at its forbidden joys.
I saw the cherub wave his flaming sword,
I knew that my rebellion was a sin;
But the old love was stronger than my fear—
It grew imperious—it mastered me;
I dashed aside the angel's lifted brand,
And here I stand, unwounded!

SOPHIA.
     And in Eden?

KÖNIGSMARK.
Close by the tree of life.

SOPHIA.
     Bold flatterer!
Countess, he talks this nonsense by the day,—
He ever talked it. You must not suppose
The man as empty as his words imply.
He has good metal in his character,
If you dig deep enough.

KÖNIGSMARK.
        Thus have I been
Game for this lady from my earliest day.
She chased me round the garden, and stuck burrs
In my long hair, when we were both at Zell;
But then I always laughed at her wild hunts,
As I do now.

SOPHIA.
      Beseech you, Countess, hark!
Lest there be aught that's treason to the Prince
In our discourse. Here is a specimen
Of that bad intercourse on which my lord
Is pleased to found his jealousy. Ah, me!
Philip, they say you are a naughty boy;
In proof of which, who was your lady-love,
This morning, in the garden?

KÖNIGSMARK.
         Countess Platen;
But keep it quiet; for the Countess says
That the Elector has distinguished me
By his august and gracious jealousy,
Through dearth of higher favors. It may be;
But I half doubt it.

SOPHIA.
    It may be!

KÖNIGSMARK.
        Nay, nay;
It might have been.

SOPHIA.
   Indeed? But let that go:

I have no right to scrutinize your life,
Blaming this action, praising that.

KÖNIGSMARK.
      Oh! yes;
I'll thank you for the thought you waste on me.
I ill deserve the goodness of your blame;
Your praise would dizzy me. But do not think
That the least figment of what you call love
E'er passed between us. There was dazzling fence
Of wit, of spurious passion, skill and craft,
Betwixt us veteran sworders; but the foils
Wore buttons, and the conflict was all play,
We both knew well, though fighting with such heat
That the spectators thought us serious.

SOPHIA.
They say you won.

KÖNIGSMARK.
    I know but this; I won,
As the grand issue, her eternal hate.

SOPHIA.
How did you meet?

KÖNIGSMARK.
   By accident, she said.

SOPHIA.
It cost me dearly.

KÖNIGSMARK.
   You?

SOPHIA.

     His Highness saw
You and the Countess fleeing from this spot,
And in the grass he found a glove of mine,
And drew his own conclusions.

KÖNIGSMARK.

        But the glove,
How came it here?

SOPHIA.

     I lost it yesterday;
The Countess found it; and in hastening hence,
In her confusion, dropped it.

KÖNIGSMARK.

        In her craft,
This trap was laid and set to tangle you:
I see it all; and now I can account
For her strange conduct. Part by part, I take
This dainty mechanism of her brain
To pieces; and throughout I see her hand
As plain, as in the petals of this rose,
Whose combination forms the perfect flower,
I witness Nature. Lest I judge amiss,
The thorn convinces sharply. I shall blow
Her blooming prospects to the winds of heaven!

SOPHIA.

They'll not believe you. I have been refused
Credit upon my oath. A criminal's
Stoutest denial is no proof at law;
Confession only is received from him.
But I have suffered so much by my trial,

That I will not bide sentence, if my flight
To Cousin Anthony may shelter me
From the impending doom.

KÖNIGSMARK.
Hist! hist!

(*Re-enter* COUNTESS VON PLATEN.)

COUNTESS VON PLATEN.
Good-day,
Fair Princess,—and to you, sweet Count! I see
The rose has bloomed at last. (*Apart to him.*)

SOPHIA.
You're welcome, Countess.
Philip and I were wrangling. I maintained
The bread and milk my mother made in Zell
Was better than the wine of Hanover—
The fiery wine you rouse your sins withal—
Better, because more innocent, But he
Has spoiled his palate with your biting drink,
And argues otherwise. You'll make report
Of this grave matter to the Prince, no doubt.

COUNTESS VON PLATEN.
I am no gossip.

SOPHIA.
Not without a cause.
Know you this glove?

COUNTESS VON PLATEN.
I've seen it on your hand.

SOPHIA.
Where did you find it!

COUNTESS VON PLATEN.
I! I found it not.

KÖNIGSMARK.
Where did you drop it, Countess?

COUNTESS VON PLATEN.
Bless my wits!
I am besieged with questions. Gentle folks,
I came not hither to be catechised;
Nor am I skilled in tracing stolen goods
By conjuration.

KÖNIGSMARK.
Parried well! In faith,
Equivocation is as good as truth,
When simple ears are listening.

COUNTESS VON PLATEN.
Königsmark,
You may be sorry for your brutal jokes
At one, whose only fault has been regard
For your coarse, worthless self. As for your Highness,
Your lot in life is, I suppose, above
Our mortal sufferings; like the gods of old,
Nectar's your drink, ambrosia your food,
And every change of sun and moon and star,
But shows a new phase of your happiness.

SOPHIA.

Oh! I could weep for pity, at the part
You choose to play in my sad history.

COUNTESS VON PLATEN.

In truth, your judgment errs. Your own belief
Makes enemies of persons who would think
'Twere almost sacrilege to wish you ill.
Count Königsmark comes nearer to my rank,
And so I scold him, with a playful wrath,
For his misdeeds. I love you both indeed,
More than your hearts seem willing to permit.
You doubt it? Try me; that is all I ask
For your conviction.

KÖNIGSMARK.

Countess, mark this ring,
A clear-set cameo. On the under side,
You see how smooth the polished surface lies,
How veined with graceful lines, how exquisite!
But hold it thus, against God's piercing light,
And fierce Medusa's head comes staring through—
Each hair a serpent, awful as the scowl
O'er which it writhes. In ancient days, they say,
This dreadful visage turned a man to stone;
But now Medusa combs her serpents down
To wanton ringlets, smooths her threatening brow,
Smiles with her mouth, looks coyly with her eyes,
And woos the incautious mortal to her side.
Believe her not; for at some dismal hour
She'll reassume her terrors, and transform
The trusting fool to marble. Let us walk

Together towards the palace, friend with friend;
Holding our hearts as steady as we can,
Lest on the way our brimming love should spill,
And scorch the helpless flowers on either side.

         [Exeunt.

ACT IV.

SCENE. *A State Apartment in the Palace.* The ELECTOR *discovered sitting in Council, surrounded by* COUNT VON PLATEN *and other Counselors*, PRINCE MAX, BAUMAIN, *Officers, Pages, Guards, etc.*

ELECTOR.

Break up the council. Where is Königsmark?
Son Max, your handsome friend is strayed away.
Have you not seen him?

PRINCE MAX.

Please your Highness, yes;
I saw him riding a well-jaded horse,
Covered with mud and dust from head to tail,
Towards the new stables.

ELECTOR.

Whither has he been?

PRINCE MAX.

Making a foray on the country-girls,
To stock the town with. He has added you,
Heaven knows how many, to the population
Of this electoral city; not to count
The many souls that he has sent below,
To swell hell's myriads. His zeal is great.
You, and the devil, owe him many thanks
For his hot industry.

ELECTOR.

            'Tis dangerous
To make inquiries of you, graceless boy!

PRINCE MAX.

I talk my best. I do not pick my phrase
To suit the hearing of well-mannered vice.
If all things vile were called by their right names,
We'd have less preaching. 'Tis the gloss of sin
In which men see their faces, and look pleased;
Remove the varnish, and the rough, coarse grain
Would draw scant praises. When I open church,
I shall begin by giving every sin
His name according to his pedigree,
Not his new title that shames Satan's tail
In length and involution. Men may wince,
And blush, and raise their hands, and cry, "For shame!"
But till their morals bear their manners out,
I'll call a foul thing—slut!

ELECTOR.

            'Ods mercy, Max!
Is Madam Wreyké your inspiring muse?

PRINCE MAX.

I am no better than the rest of you:—
No, father, I am worse; for I have bowed
My natural temper to abhorred desires,
And, like a youthful drunkard, crazed myself
With draughts revolting to my palate's taste.
I've not attained to self-deception, though:
There's your last step in guilt.

      (*Enter* COUNTESS VON PLATEN.)

                    Max, Max, my son,
You are a strange and inconsistent boy;
Having one grain of goodness mixed in you
With every ounce of ill. I sometimes think
That Nature meant you for a parish priest,
But used you for a prince; there's such a jar
Betwixt your heart and fortune. Credit me,
I love you well, madcap philosopher,—
Your naughty holiness, I love you well!

     PRINCE MAX.
I know it, father.

    (*Enter* KÖNIGSMARK.)
     ELECTOR.
   Ah! Count Königsmark!
'Twere breach of state to say I wait for you,
Though something near the truth. You seem
 fatigued.

     KÖNIGSMARK.
Unwonted exercise has jaded me.
I took an early gallop from the town,
And lost my way. That has belated me;
For which I crave your Highness' pardon.

     ELECTOR.
      Count,
The doctors tell me travel is a thing
As wholesome to the body as the mind.

     KÖNIGSMARK.
I was about to ask your Highness leave
To visit Paris.

ELECTOR.

     Paris, by all means ;—
Rome, Athens, Cairo, Pekin and Bombay,
The South Sea Islands, Lima, Mexico,
The land that freezes to the Northern Pole,
And the wide prairies of America,
Were not amiss, perhaps. And mark you, Count,
I purpose that you travel round and round
My little Hanover for many years,
Settling its boundaries surely in your mind,
Ere you re-enter it. You understand?

KÖNIGSMARK.

My banishment!

ELECTOR.

     Oh no; for you shall have
Your usual pension from the public purse
Doubled; and I'll so manage your affairs,
That all the property you leave behind
Shall yield a large increase of revenue.
Banished! you're favored. As a special mark
Of my regard, my son, Prince Maximilian,
Shall travel with you. He has pressing need
To rummage through the world in search of wit;
Even if the quest should put some leagues of land
'Twixt him and Madam Wreyké. You must start—
I give you leisure to prepare, you see—
To-morrow morning; for my eager Max
Waxes impatient.

PRINCE MAX.

    Please, your Highness—

ELECTOR.
                    Yes;
Your plans of travel please my Highness well
But I will hear no more about it, sirs;
Your long discourse grows tedious. I hate
Long stories, and long women, and long faces,
More than an ague.

COUNTESS VON PLATEN.
              He has sprung a mine
Under my feet, and sent my secret works
In fragments to the moon. Well done, old sin!
But now to countermine. (*Aside.*)   [*Exit.*

ELECTOR.
          Are you content?

PRINCE MAX.
Perforce, I am.

ELECTOR.
          And you, Count?

KÖNIGSMARK.
                  Your command
Goes with my heart. I have outstayed my time,
It seems, and welcome changes to farewell;
But that is better than to be thrust forth,
Against all hospitable rites. Heaven knows,
I was unconscious of your Highness' wish
Before it fell so harshly on my ears.
My heart has talons, clinging where it loves,
But, oh! my pride has wings. Take back your gifts
Of rank and money; they but measured out
Your favor to me—tokens of a love

Which they but represented: in themselves
As mean as is a banker's paper bill,
That stands for something which itself is not.
The debt is canceled, and the bill erased;
I scatter it in fragments to the wind:
The thing is worthless. From your Hanover
I will not draw a penny, though grim want
With his lean fingers pinch my empty purse.
My lands, my houses and my equipage,
Before another day grow old, shall shake
Beneath the mallet of the auctioneer,
Though every blow be ruin.

ELECTOR.
      Königsmark,
Pride's a poor reasoner: think.

KÖNIGSMARK.
      I dare not think,
Lest base temptations overcome my soul.
Urge me no more. I have one precious jewel,
That, leaving all things, I would carry hence,
As a safe talisman against regret—
My self-respect. While that remains to me,
What sordid Plutus, from his money-bags,
Shall dare to call me poor?

PRINCE MAX.
      By Jupiter,
Here's one deserves the royal name of man!
Go boot and saddle for our travel, Count!
We'll wear the hills to valleys with our feet,
Before I leave you, if so high a soul
Will take so low a comrade.

KÖNIGSMARK.

You are more—
Far more than generous in your thoughts of me:
His Highness will provide you better friends.
For I must break all holds with Hanover;
I would not have my memory linked to it
Even through your love, Prince Max. I take my leave,
Your Highness, with the promise that to-morrow
Shall make us strangers.

ELECTOR.

Choose your time. Farewell,
Thou hot but noble spirit! If a friend
May e'er have leave to serve you, do me right,
And look to Hanover; for she may be
A kingdom ere you think.

(*As* KÖNIGSMARK *is going, enter* SOPHIA.)

KÖNIGSMARK.

(*Apart to her.*) I've seen the Duke.
This letter from him will explain the rest.
In heaven's name, Princess, ere you take your flight,
Contrive that we may meet! (*Gives a letter, which she conceals, and Exit.*)

ELECTOR.

What said the Count?

SOPHIA.

Oh! much in little—"Good-day" and "Farewell."

ELECTOR

Max, you will please me, if you give no note

Of Königsmark's departure. (*Apart to him.*)
[*Exit* PRINCE MAX.

SOPHIA.

     I am come
Upon a painful errand to your Highness.
But, lest I do injustice to your son,
Call in Prince George.

ELECTOR.

    Your husband? You may call
In thunder to him, and he will not hear.
Surely you know he's half-way to Berlin,
To spend a fortnight.

SOPHIA.

     No; in his designs
I am no partner. But I shall not pause
To broach the matter. I am come prepared
With simple statements, that make no attempt
To move by eloquence. Dry logic, facts,
That lie within the sight of every one,
Are all I offer. I shall make no charge
To wrong my absent husband, nor disarm
His due defence by any forward blow.
Let him accuse himself. I, for my part,
Speak only for myself.

ELECTOR.

     I always said
You were half angel. You are vexed, I guess,
At George's jealousy; but jealousy
Proves love.

SOPHIA.

        Ah! yes; and parceling out his heart
Among a crowd of women, lest its weight
Distress the lawful bearer of the load,
That too proves love! You treat me as a child
Whom you would woo, not punish. I demand
The culprit's trial and the culprit's doom,
If I am guilty. If you find me true,
I ask redress in a just, lawful way—
Such rights accorded as befit my wrongs;
And I will have them from your Highness' hand,
Or snatch them with my own.

ELECTOR.

                      Your anger speaks.
I'll not deny some justice in your words;
But justice is not always wisdom, dear.
There's many a wife who suffers more than you,
Yet makes the best of it, and glides along
As smoothly as the average of wives.
Your opposition to the current's set
Stirs up the storm, and blinds your eyes with spray.
Swim with the stream.

SOPHIA.

               I cannot; let me drown;
The baseness of the struggle frenzies me.
What if I live through degradation, wrong,
Brutality, and, half a century hence,
Land on the fairest slope of Paradise?
For my best comfort, I should save a soul
Not worth the saving—a dejected thing,
To slouch and tremble at the gaze of Heaven
Throughout an immortality of shame.

ELECTOR.

Bah! you talk nonsense. Hanover and Zell,
A wedded kingdom, to descend to you,
And follow to your children.—There's a view
To reconcile you to your high-perched home,
And make its damps and solitudes look gay.

SOPHIA.

Were I the lowest corner of those lands,
You would not let them tread my verdure out,
And plant me full of nettles, in your sight.
Will you do nothing?

ELECTOR.
     What thing can I do?

SOPHIA.
Divorce me from my husband.

ELECTOR.
       Holy saints!
Put Zell and Hanover apart again!
The thought is madness.

SOPHIA.
      You must clearly see
The mutual misery in which we live.—

ELECTOR.
See! I see nothing but poor Hanover,
A crownless dukedom, with its empty hands
Stretched towards disdainful Zell—a woeful sight!

SOPHIA.
So, then, I am not spirit, flesh and blood,

An aching heart, a bitter memory,
A living, breathing, conscious human thing;
But leagues of level country, stocks and stones,
Houses and beggars' hovels, pens and styes,
To be transferred by charter, and feel proud
That my lord deigns to put his careless foot,
Sometimes, upon my bosom!

ELECTOR

Such a lot,
As hers who represents my Zell to me,
Is not unhonored. Daughter, at a bound,
You overleap the barriers of life,
That cramp the lowly, and become a star
To fix the eyes of nations. Ay, a star
With a grand orbit, a far-reaching force,
Controlling planets; but no less a part
Of a great system, to whose central law
It is your duty to conform yourself.

SOPHIA.

I find small honor and great misery
In such a portion. 'Tis a woman's whim
To pine for freedom; but I'd rather be
My poor heart's mistress than the world's.

ELECTOR.

Poh! poh!
You talk at random. Put your trust in me;
And when the crown of Hanover and Zell
Rests on your forehead, you will count me wise.

SOPHIA.

Then, Heaven, direct me! I have made appeal

To my last earthly succor. Your reply
Touches my grief no nigher than the sounds
Of some triumphal festival the ear
Of a lone mother, hugging her starved babe
Closer, to let the mocking show go by.
What is the crown of Hanover and Zell
To me, who feel the martyr's fiery ring
Pinching my temples? Hanover and Zell!—
A drop of honey to a starving wretch—
A spark to one who freezes! Will your Highness
Talk of such tinsel, while my awful woe
Sits on her throne, and laughs at your poor tricks?
Call me a child; but I'm a dying child;
And if you offer toys, I'll put them by,
Not with the child's sweet tyranny, perhaps,
But somewhat rudely.

ELECTOR.

     I shall speak with George—
By Heaven, and I will do it in a way
To make the boy remember! Shall my plans—
Your father's too—miscarry in the end,
Because the brute who bears them goes astray?
The hopes of Hanover, of Germany.—
For mark you, this is but our first great step
Towards a grand union of the German States
Into one mighty nation. Think of that!
Do you suppose that interests such as these
Shall go to ruin for a pink-faced girl,
Who whines and whimpers, with or without cause,
Because it is her nature? Marry, now,
It makes me angry! But that headstrong boy,
Who will not bear the yoke, shall feel the goad,
And mend his paces.

SOPHIA.

     That is naught to me:
You cannot patch up injury with wrath.
He has accused me in a public place,
Before the face of man, before my face,
With that gross crime, of which I only know
Because it is his practice.

ELECTOR.

      Fool, blind fool!
He'll bruise his knees before you for this act.

SOPHIA.

If I am guilty, I am unworthy of him;
If innocent, he is unworthy of me.
I'll take my leave, your Highness, and prepare,
With Heaven's assistance, for the dismal days
That frown before me.

ELECTOR.

     That is right, my child:
Lean hard on heaven, and it will bear you up.
There's no harm done by praying; but take care
That you pray softly to yourself, not loud,
Lest other ears than Heaven's receive your prayers,
And do us mischief. Low and earnest prayer—
I always preached that in my bishopric,
When I taught doctrine to my little flock,—
In which the wolves and goats made up the mass,
The sheep and lambs being scanty. But of that
We will say nothing. It was long ago:
Perhaps the world has mended.

SOPHIA.

      My low prayers

Shall not forget your Highness. You have shown
A heart that's only warped by statesmancraft
From a right purpose. I have seen you hide
A pity brimming in your eyes for me
Beneath your robe of office. I'll not blame
That which, perchance, my ignorance condemns;
Nor set my sorrow up against the claim
Which Hanover holds on you. If you prize
The gratitude of one, left fatherless
By slippery fortune, take it in God's name!—
I cast it towards you with my whole full heart!
                                  [*Exit.*

                ELECTOR.

When Königsmark is gone, and some small sense
Of decency is hammered through the head
Of mulish George, Sophia may begin
To look on life with better favor. 'Sdeath!
These aching hearts that long for sympathy,
With sentimental loves, and hates, and woes,
For all their softness, are the toughest stuff
That I e'er worked in. I am plagued with hearts—
With other people's driveling, senseless hearts:
Hearts are my devils. If I take a step,
I am sure to stumble over one of them.
My heart! your heart!—Why, 'tis the fool's excuse
For all his folly, and the hypocrite's
Grand plea for all his selfishness. The eye
Drops tears upon it, but it will not feel—
The reason pricks it, but it will not move—
Experience warns it, but it will not hear—
Truth shines upon it, but it will not see—
Sense gives it dainties, but it will not taste—
And plucks it roses, but it will not smell:

And so, poor head, thou art but deputy
To a dumb maniac, and thy policy
Hangs on the changes of the wandering moon.

(*Re-enter* COUNTESS VON PLATEN.)

COUNTESS VON PLATEN.

Your Highness.—

ELECTOR.

Well, Elizabeth, how now?
Have you come here to vex me with your heart?
I wish you had none.

COUNTESS VON PLATEN.

I have little heart—

ELECTOR.

That's cheering.

COUNTESS VON PLATEN.

I have little heart, I say,
To tell the reason of my coming.

ELECTOR.

Well?
I'm listening with both ears.

COUNTESS VON PLATEN.

You recollect
That you once bade me to trace out the bond
Betwixt the Princess and Count Königsmark.—

ELECTOR.

Bade you! forbade you, rather; but agreed,
At length, to grant your curious desire,
For peace' sake and precaution.

COUNTESS VON PLATEN.

      Let that pass;
It matters little. I have traced it out,
And find it—

ELECTOR.

  What?

COUNTESS VON PLATEN.

  Love.

ELECTOR.

     Love! more hearts! Ye gods,
I shall go crazy! Proof, proof, proof, I say,
Before my wits turn over!

COUNTESS VON PLATEN.

      Proof? nay, facts.
Count Königsmark will visit her to-night
In her own chamber.

ELECTOR.

     Nonsense! You all plot
To rob me of my Zell, my darling Zell,
Whose flat, plain face is fairer in my eyes
Than Rubens' Flora.

COUNTESS VON PLATEN.

     George's jealousy
Was not a dream.

ELECTOR.

     My life is all a dream,—
A hideous nightmare! Hanover and Zell
Dreamt they were wedded, and awake, to find

Themselves at daggers' points. For pity's sake,
How came you by this rubbish?

COUNTESS VON PLATEN.
        Ask me not:
I am bound to secresy.

ELECTOR.
      And I am bound,
By my incredulous nature, to believe
Nothing I hear, and only half I see.

COUNTESS VON PLATEN.
Issue a warrant for the Count's arrest;
And in the private audit he shall have,
You may both hear and see.

ELECTOR.
       You're confident.

COUNTESS VON PLATEN.
It is too certain, Ernest. I would doubt
But cannot: there's no shift for unbelief.
Issue the warrant.

ELECTOR.
    Take it then.

COUNTESS VON PLATEN.
        Not now:
We must arrest him in the very act,
With guilt upon him.

ELECTOR.
      Take him from her room,
And fill the world with scandal! No, no, no!

If Königsmark be guilty, he shall suffer,
But not in public; nor shall any cause
Be offered for his fate. Sophia's character
Must be kept spotless, for my kingdom's sake.
I'll strike the evil at the very spring.
Remove this Königsmark, and she, perforce,
Must settle down to virtue. If she's false,
The fault is in her heart, not in her blood,
And, therefore, curable.

COUNTESS VON PLATEN.

Well, have your will:
Though, to my simple judgment, it appears
Something like tyranny to punish guilt
Without a trial. For unless you act
As I have counseled, you will have no proof,
And thus no trial.

ELECTOR.

True.

COUNTESS VON PLATEN.

But if he's seized
Within her chamber, or just issuing thence,
Or at safe distance—so the fact stand clear—
What can he say to help him? Not a word.
He'll die, unshriven, to shield his paramour,
And, by his silence, save Sophia's fame.

ELECTOR.

You'd not cry murder till the deed is done,
But I would fain prevent it. Why should he
Have access to her chamber?

COUNTESS VON PLATEN.
                    What of that?
He has been there before.

           ELECTOR.
                    Elizabeth,
That's sweet morality!

           COUNTESS VON PLATEN.
                    Morality!
Pish, Ernest, pish! It seems to me, of late,
That you have left the line of policy,
And struck out a new pathway straight for heaven.
Heaven speed you then! (*Going.*)

           ELECTOR.
           Where shall we seize the Count?
Not in her chamber?

           COUNTESS VON PLATEN.
           Where you please. This thing
Has little personal regard from me.
I care not if you let the Count escape:
He is no enemy of mine. The girl
I care no more for than a painted doll;—
Save that she holds your Zell in trust for you,
And that will not be periled.

           ELECTOR.
                    Let me see:
Not in her chamber, nor the corridor;
For there the guard would understand the cause.—
Ay!—now I have it—in the Ritter's Hall.

To cross that hall were damning; for the way
Lies through her chamber.—In the Ritter's Hall.

COUNTESS VON PLATEN.

Well, have you settled it? Pray, think again.

ELECTOR.

No; that were best.

COUNTESS VON PLATEN.

                But who shall manage it?
It will not do to trust in any one.

ELECTOR.

No, no; nor must the soldiers of the guard
Suspect me in the business; else the weight
So strangely thrown into a mere arrest,
Would set them thinking. Dear Elizabeth,
I'll ask a favor of you. (*Writing.*) Here's the warrant.

COUNTESS VON PLATEN.

What shall I do with it?

ELECTOR.

                Why, see it served.

COUNTESS VON PLATEN.

I!

ELECTOR.

  You.

COUNTESS VON PLATEN.

    Excuse me. You forget my sex.

ELECTOR.

Do you forget it, for my sake.

COUNTESS VON PLATEN.

          O Lord!
This is grim jesting, Ernest!

ELECTOR.

                    I can trust
This handsome villain to your hands, I know:
You have a taste for manly beauty.—Nay;
They say you one time held Count Königsmark
In high esteem—ah, Bess!

COUNTESS VON PLATEN.

                    When I begin
To stop court-scandal, you shall have a share
In my wide business; for I know of none
More deeply interested. Do you mean
That I shall really take Count Königsmark,
And on this warrant? (*Taking it.*)

ELECTOR.

          Yes. Baumain is safe—
A trusty fellow;—let him do the deed
By your direction. But no blood must flow.
O'erpower the Count with numbers; bring him here,
Swiftly and silently. I'll judge his case
According to the facts. How sad this is!
For Königsmark would leave us to ourselves
To-morrow morning, and so end it all.
Perhaps, 'twere well to shut our eyes again,
And let him go unquestioned.

COUNTESS VON PLATEN.

                    As you said,
Ernest, that's sweet morality!

ELECTOR.

                                Indeed,
I have no wish to enter on this work ;
My heart misgives me. Duty, duty, though ;
I must remember that. You'll see it done?

COUNTESS VON PLATEN.

Yes, as a woman may. But if I err,
Through want of judgment, you must pardon me.

ELECTOR.

Deal gently with him—that is all. No blood—
Remember that—no butchery, to fill
Our crazy palace with fresh walking ghosts.

COUNTESS VON PLATEN.

He'll not resist your warrant, surely.

ELECTOR.

                                       No,
I think he will not; but his blood is hot,
And his hand hankers for his sword, I've marked,
When aught opposes him. Be circumspect.

COUNTESS VON PLATEN.

I shall ; for gentleness, at least, should guide
A woman's ministration of the law.

ELECTOR.

Adieu ! I'll watch for you and Königsmark
In the blue chamber.—But no noise, no noise.
Adieu, Elizabeth !   [*Exit.*

COUNTESS VON PLATEN.

            No noise, no noise !

What if he shriek? The cry will haunt my ears,
And drown the pleasant sounds of earth for ever.
Pshaw! he's a man; he will not shriek, I know.
What if he struggle—beg for mercy—yield?—
Shall I relent? Oh Heaven! one hideous sight
Paints all my fancy! it is Königsmark—
His fair face hacked—his bosom red with blood—
His filmy eyes rolled upward against heaven,
In fearful wonder, staring for the soul
Just parted from them. Shall I— Ha! to mock
My growing weakness, see, the man draws nigh,
Swelling with insolent arrogance; his lips
Curling with sneers and insults that defy
My feeble menaces, and scorn my love.
Remorse can have no agonies to match
The gnawing teeth of unappeased revenge!
                                           [*Exit.*
      (*Re-enter* KÖNIGSMARK.)

KÖNIGSMARK.

I feel like one who, dying, turning his eyes
Towards every corner of his narrow room,
And picks each object out, as though he sought
To bear their memory to the other world.
I roam the palace without aim; yet still,
As each familiar thing stands in my view,
I greet it kindly, and with melting eyes
Bid it farewell, almost unconsciously.
Grief clouds my mind: I cannot realize
The parting happiness, nor coming ill.
A dreamy torpor hangs upon my sense,
And, like the mercy in a deadly blow,
Stuns ere it kills. If any one had said,
The Princess will not grieve to see you go;

She will not even grant you the poor rite,
Which etiquette enjoins on severing friends,
To say farewell; I should have smiled in scorn
From the high summit of my confidence.
Yet so it seems. I've sought her far and near;
But even where we idly loitered once,
And spun the time out, merely for the sake
Of keeping back our parting,—now, alas!
In my most pressing want, I find her not.
Ah! let the mortal, wise in his own thought,
Look through thy darkened glass, Adversity,
If he would see the truthful hue of life,
And know it as it is!

(*Enter a* PAGE.)

PAGE.

Count Königsmark.

KÖNIGSMARK.

Well, sir?—He wears the Princess' livery. (*Aside.*)
What is your errand?

PAGE.

Nothing more than this.
(*Gives him a note and exit.*)

KÖNIGSMARK. (*Reading.*)

Oh! I misjudged her! In her chamber, ha!
At one o'clock to-night! Strange, very strange!
"I need fear nothing; Countess Knesebeck
Will stay in hearing." Ah, sweet innocent!
Or does she jest with me? Boy!—he is gone.
Oh! golden sunset to a stormy day!

The west breaks out in splendor! Why should I
Pine for the rising, while the setting sun
Shines on me thus? Night follows, and not day.
True; but the night may cover me with stars,
And rain down blessings from her peaceful breast!
[*Exit.*

ACT V.

SCENE I. *The Chamber of the Princess.* COUNTESS VON KNESE-BECK *discovered. Enter* SOPHIA, *weeping.*

SOPHIA.

Well, it is over.

COUNTESS VON KNESEBECK.

What?

SOPHIA.

My agony;
The greatest anguish that a mother's heart
Can bear, unbroken. Parting from a child,
That goes to seek its little happiness
With some young playfellow, or distant friend,
For a short season, draws a mother's tears;
What should I do, whose comfort is bare hope
In the blind future? Sense cannot express,
Words have no passion for a grief like mine.
If I were dying, mere necessity,
And helpless yielding to supreme command,
Might fix my soul; but here the choice is mine.
I calmly forfeit motherhood, to shun
The evils that surround it. Countess, think,
What fearful sufferings must have been the lot—
Suppose it what you may—that could compel
A loving mother to this dread extreme.

COUNTESS VON KNESEBECK.

Take comfort, Princess; you may see your children

In Brunswick, sometimes; or Duke Anthony
May make such stipulations, on your part,
That your return to them may be secure.

SOPHIA.

You talk of possibilities, and I
Want certainties before I go. The wretch
Who casts her babe to a pursuing wolf,
For her own safety, may pray angry Heaven
To save the child, or hope some hunter's shot
Will come between the savage and his prey;
But would you, therefore, hold the coward free
From just contempt?

COUNTESS VON KNESEBECK.

     You push the case too far:
You do not jeopardize your children's lives
By your hard flight.

SOPHIA.

    I jeopardize their souls;
I make them o'er to strangers who shall teach
Their lips to curse me.—Oh! those taintless lips,
That now pray for me, wiping, at a breath,
The grievous record 'twixt myself and Heaven
As white as snow. I saw them as they lay,
Nestled together in their narrow bed,
Cheek against cheek—one pillow served them both—
And their bright hair was tangled so in one,
My eyes could not divide it. The deep flush
Of infant slumber burned on George's cheeks,
And centred in the crimson of his lips,
That smiled on guilty me. That joyful smile

Ran, like good tidings, through the realm of dreams;
For now his sister smiled, and stretched her arms,
And murmured "Mother!" Unless Heaven should plead,
There is no eloquence to hold me here
So strongly as that word. I laughed and wept—
I kissed them both—I hugged them to my heart—
And then—what think you?—then I said farewell!

COUNTESS VON KNESEBECK.

Oh, Heaven! oh, Heaven!

SOPHIA.

Weep, if you can, poor friend:
My tear-drops, like the petrifying tide
Of the Italian lake, turned me to stone;
And now the branch, that bent with every breeze,
Is fixed as marble. I shall not relent.
Go pack the clothes I brought with me from Zell;
Their style is old, but I will not take hence
A thread of Hanover. And in my desk,
You'll find a little store of Zellish gold:
'Twill be enough; and it is mine—my own;
I drew it from my father's treasury.
All that is Hanover's I'll leave behind,
And with it, by God's grace, my misery.

[*Exit* COUNTESS VON KNESEBECK.

Here are my jewels; I must look to them,
And separate the gems of Hanover
From my poor trinkets. This my mother gave;
And this the Prince, when little George was born.—
O children, children, if you only knew
What the flight costs the hapless fugitive,

You would not blame me, as perhaps you will.
Rest here, proud jewel; let the giver take,
And reckon me above his charity.
Elector, there's your necklace. Mother-in-law,
Here is your diadem come back again!
This a birth-day ring poor Philip gave—
      (*Knock at the door.*)
Come in, come in.
    (*Enter* KÖNIGSMARK.)
    What, Countess, back so soon?
I would not lose this ring: I'll try it on.
Why, how my hand has grown since this was given!
Philip was vexed, because it was too large—
Poor Philip—

    KÖNIGSMARK.
  Ay, poor Philip!

    SOPHIA.
      Ha! you here!
What mean you by this folly? Königsmark,
Have you gone crazy? What induces you
To hazard fame for me, life for yourself,
By this rash visit? Speak, what brings you here?

    KÖNIGSMARK.
Your note.
    SOPHIA.
  My note! I never sent you one.

    KÖNIGSMARK.
Read it. I know your characters too well,
To doubt that note. (*Gives it.*)

SOPHIA.

It is a forgery:
I did not write a syllable of this.

KÖNIGSMARK.

Alas! I hoped you did.

SOPHIA.

And well you might.
We are entrapped. This note was surely forged
To bring you hither; but the end's not yet,
Though close upon us, doubtless. Stand you there,
With ruin all around us? Königsmark,
The forgers of this paper have designed
To take you in my chamber. Every minute
That you remain, gives opportunity.
In Heaven's name, will you go?

KÖNIGSMARK.

No!

SOPHIA.

Be it so:
I'll take destruction, if you offer it;
But it is hard to credit, that your hand
Can do such service for my enemies.

KÖNIGSMARK.

I am here; you say our foes are at the door;
They shall not pass it. (*Bolts the door.*)

SOPHIA.

Philip, are you mad?

KÖNIGSMARK.

No; I act wisely. Ere they find me here,

I'll leap from yonder window, though quick death
Look upward at me from the depth below.
I have somewhat I must say; I shall be brief;
And if you e'er recall my words, remember
They were my last.

SOPHIA.
How so?

KÖNIGSMARK.
To-morrow, Princess,
I quit your sight for ever.

SOPHIA.
What?

KÖNIGSMARK.
Perhaps,
You have not heard that I am banished.

SOPHIA.
No—
No, indeed, Philip—this is news to me.
Banished for what?

KÖNIGSMARK.
For your sake, I suppose,
Though 'twas not mentioned.

SOPHIA.
Ha! ha! what a slip
These cunning people make! To-night, I too
Quit Hanover for ever.

KÖNIGSMARK.
You!

I

SOPHIA.

       Yes, yes.
In Brunswick, Philip, we may meet again;
Where friendship may not be, as here it is,
Reckoned among our crimes. Duke Anthony
Invites me, instantly, to come to him;
And for that purpose, he has set at Piend
An escort to receive me.

KÖNIGSMARK.

       Be not rash.
I fear you have not counted the effect
Of this bold purpose on your happiness.

SOPHIA.

My husband has prepared me for the worst
By one last action. Listen! Ere he left,
With the alacrity of shame, and fled,
To hide his baseness in Berlin, we two
Had an encounter of high, stormy words;
In which he thundered, and I only rained,
As is my sex's habit. Towards the last,
Heated with wine and anger, in gross terms,
He charged me with a crime which he himself
Knew, as he uttered it, to be a lie.
My spirit, hitherto as meek as grief
And nervous fear could make it, rose at this;
And, in plain words, I called the odious taunt
By its right name—I called it a foul lie!
How do you think he answered?—With a blow!
Struck me, a princess—nay, a woman, man!—
Are you not blushing for your paltry sex?

See here, the seal of his high infamy
'Gainst God and Nature, reddens on my throat,
Where his vile hand affixed it!

KÖNIGSMARK.

       Coward!—brute!
In vindication of all manhood, stained
From surface unto centre, I shall call
The heartless ruffian to account for this.

SOPHIA.

Oh, no; he has the right, the right by law,
Founded on man's best wisdom. Every code,
Made by your Dracos, sanctions deeds like his.
But shall I, if the Lord has given me strength
And limbs to crawl away, stay here till blows
Have made them useless?

KÖNIGSMARK.

      No; away, away!
What man shall blame you, when your story's told,
Or make a motion on your husband's part?

SOPHIA.

All men, I fear; but I shall venture it,
Relying on Heaven's judgment more than man's.
Philip, farewell! When I am safe in Brunswick,
We may be friends beneath a brighter sky.
That strange note frightened me; and yet I see
No reason for alarm. Some would-be wit
Sent it, perhaps, in silly merriment.
I do not blame him; though 'twere dangerous,
If he were lurking to o'erlook his trick.

KÖNIGSMARK.

I quite forgot the note, the time, the place.
All places seem as one, when you are near;
All times seem late enough, when we must part;
And who shall charge me with ingratitude
Towards any chance that brings me to your side?

SOPHIA.

There, Philip, there! in raptures once again!
Your gallantry is endless. Leave me now.

KÖNIGSMARK.

Hear me! I love you.—

SOPHIA.

                Is it generous
To air your humors at a time like this?

KÖNIGSMARK.

Thus have you parried me, and put to shame
My modest homage, more than once before.
You will not understand me; or you feign
To think me jesting when I speak in truth.
I ask no answer from you. My high love
Is also generous, and would not see
Your spirit humbled. Make me no reply,
By word, or motion, or confessing blush:
But I will speak. The mean hypocrisy
Of secret worship galls my self-respect:
I feel as though a crime were on my soul.
If I have wronged you by my stealthy love,
Let me endure the open punishment:
I shall feel happier.

SOPHIA.

           Philip Königsmark,
This is all wrong. To me 'tis cruelty—
Most wanton cruelty. You would erase
Those blameless feelings which my heart has kept
Through every trial,—that fair memory
Which made the thought of you inseparable
From home and childhood, and array yourself
Against my virtue, as a dangerous man
To be suspected, watched and held at bay.
Henceforth, I shall not trust you as of old;
I shall not dare to look into your face,
With the calm confidence of innocence,
Lest careless trust should leave some door ajar
For ambushed love to enter. I must raise
Between us two the barriers of the world,
The guards of etiquette; and wipe away,
As a false picture of my fantasy,
The playmate children in the grounds of Zell.
Ah, 'tis a heavy sorrow! for you leave
An empty place in my ill-furnished heart,
That must remain for ever.

KÖNIGSMARK.

                You mistake:
I would not drag my idol to the ground,
And soil its lustre with my vain caress.
Remain upon your altar, safe from me,
In the dread splendor of divinity.
I do not pray, I worship. Now, farewell!
Hereafter, when you look upon my face—
Be it with joy or sorrow—you may think

What thing of me you will; but, by high Heaven,
You shall not think me false! Farewell, farewell!
(*Knock at the door.*)

SOPHIA.

Ha! we are lost!

KÖNIGSMARK.

Where does that passage lead?

SOPHIA.

Into my closet.

KÖNIGSMARK.

And I need not ask,
How many feet of empty air there are
Between yon window and the ground. Here lies
My rapid course then. (*Approaches the window.*)

SOPHIA.

Madman, hold! Hark, hark!
Listen one moment. (*Goes to the door.*) Who is
there?

COUNTESS VON KNESEBECK.

(*Without.*) 'Tis I.

SOPHIA.

It is the Countess Knesebeck—thank God!
Are you alone?

COUNTESS VON KNESEBECK.

(*Without.*) Yes, Princess.

SOPHIA.

No one near?
Can you see no one in the corridor?
Look sharply.

COUNTESS VON KNESEBECK.

(*Without.*) No; all is as still as death.

KÖNIGSMARK.

As death! my inmost spirit echoes that. (*Aside.*)

SOPHIA.

Go bring my traveling-cloak and quilted hood;
I left them in the nursery.

COUNTESS VON KNESEBECK.

(*Without.*) Pray make haste;
The horses wait us.

SOPHIA.

Countess? No reply.
Now, Philip, quick! (*Opens the door.*) God bless
 you! I forgive:
I cannot part in anger from you. Here,
Here is my hand, my brother.

KÖNIGSMARK.

Gracious Heaven,
Rain blessings on her, till thy treasury
Be emptied of its bounties! As for me,
I sail into the tempest, careless now
Whether I swim or founder. [*Exit.*

SOPHIA.

Gone, gone, gone!
And yet his blessing lingers; for I feel
That Heaven draws nearer as he leaves my side,
And some mysterious power supplies his place,
And takes his office. (*Knock at the door.*)

COUNTESS VON KNESEBECK.
(*Without.*) Princess!—

SOPHIA.
Well, come in!
(*Re-enter* COUNTESS VON KNESEBECK.)

COUNTESS VON KNESEBECK.
There's some one in the corridor.

SOPHIA.
Indeed!

COUNTESS VON KNESEBECK.
I heard a step.

SOPHIA.
A fancy. Look again.

COUNTESS VON KNESEBECK.
I can see nothing. (*Looking out.*)

SOPHIA.
Do you know the time?

COUNTESS VON KNESEBBCK.
Past one.

SOPHIA.
So late? Then we are waited for.
Throw on my cloak. I'll take one farewell look
At my poor children. How my spirits sink
Before this action; but my will is firm.
Scorn, insult, blows! Such things as these have made
Self-murder sweet, and snapped the ties of life
With desperate haste. Why should I hesitate,

Who only flee, and in some happier hour,
May knit again the raveled bond between
My children and myself? Come, come, at once!
[*Exeunt.*

SCENE II. *The Ritter's Hall.* Enter COUNTESS VON PLATEN,
with a light, meeting a PAGE.

COUNTESS VON PLATEN.

You gave the note?

PAGE.

Yes, Countess.

COUNTESS VON PLATEN.

And what then?

PAGE.

I waited in the corridor since dark,
Behind a pillar, as you ordered me,
And saw the Count go by my hiding-place:
I could have touched him.

COUNTESS VON PLATEN.

He has not returned?

PAGE.

No, Countess.

COUNTESS VON PLATEN.

Are you certain?

PAGE.

Very sure.

COUNTESS VON PLATEN.

Well done, my boy! Here is a purse of gold: (*Gives
    a purse.*)
Pour out the gold, and put your tongue in it,
To keep you quiet. There's an empty cell,
Beneath the castle, where the Elector keeps
His tell-tales, Fritz: remember that. Now go!
                                     [*Exit* PAGE.
Baumain!

(*Enter* BAUMAIN, *disguised.*)

BAUMAIN.

Your ladyship?

COUNTESS VON PLATEN.

                Where are your men?

BAUMAIN.

Here, in the passage.

COUNTESS VON PLATEN.

                Have you given them wine?

BAUMAIN.

Too much, I fear; the knaves are riotous.

COUNTESS VON PLATEN.

When all is over, here's a bag of gold
To shake amongst them. (*Gives a purse.*) Hark!
    I heard a step.

BAUMAIN.

It was the casement.

COUNTESS VON PLATEN.
How it blows to-night!
We shall have rain ere morning.

BAUMAIN.
Do you think
The Count will know me thus?

COUNTESS VON PLATEN.
No.

BAUMAIN.
If the Count—

COUNTESS VON PLATEN.
How dull you are! Have I not told you all?
I'll not repeat it.

BAUMAIN.
Pardon me: you'll find
I am apt in action. If the Count should yield?

COUNTESS VON PLATEN.
He must not yield. Say nothing of the warrant—
How could he read it in the dark, forsooth?—
Keep it, I pray you, for your own defence:
That is its purpose.—Listen! I would know
That step among a thousand. It is he.
Prepare yourself. (*Exit* BAUMAIN.) Now, Philip Königsmark,
We shall break even in this last account! [*Exit.*

(*Enter* KÖNIGSMARK.)

KÖNIGSMARK.
What hangs upon my footsteps? The close night

Grows thicker here. If I could yield myself
To superstitious fancies, I might say
That, as I cross this hall, I plainly feel
The hand of some strange phantom pluck me back,
Now by the cloak—now by the sleeve—and now,
Horror! 'tis on my shoulder! Fie, this chill,
That stirs my hair and shivers down my limbs,
Is a reproach to common manliness.
Yet as I walk, it seems as though my steps
Were all repeated, with like time and sound,
By something just behind me. Oh, for shame!
A streak of day would make me laugh at this.
Where am I now? This is the Ritter's Hall:
I dimly see the banners and the arms
Hanging above me. Ugh! how damp it is,
And cold, yet close! The air feels dense and dead,
As though it had not moved for centuries,
And full of noisome odors. Faith, I feel
As though I were descending, step by step,
Into the hollow of a grizzly tomb;
The fair warm sunlight seems so far away,
And I so wretched and oppressed at heart!
I'll shake this weakness off. Where lies my way?
The door should be there, on the left-hand side.
Right; here it is.

BAUMAIN.

(*Without.*) Stand! who goes there?

KÖNIGSMARK.

                              A friend.
Thank Heaven, the voice is human! Who has set
A guard in this strange place? 'Tis something new,
And might be fatal now.

(*Re-enter* BAUMAIN *with a torch.* KÖNIGSMARK
muffles up his face.)

BAUMAIN.

Who, sir, are you,
Walking so late upon forbidden ground?

KÖNIGSMARK.

A friend, I said, and it remains with you
To keep me so.

BAUMAIN.

Your words are bold and proud.
Disclose yourself.

KÖNIGSMARK.

He is a stranger. (*Aside.*) Well?
(*Drops his cloak.*)

BAUMAIN.

I do not know your face.

KÖNIGSMARK.

Nor I yours, sooth;
Though haply, sir, your huge, uncomely beard
May hide fair features.

BAUMAIN.

Give the countersign.

KÖNIGSMARK.

The countersign! Good fellow, let me know
Who set you here upon this novel guard?

BAUMAIN.

I was not set to answer questions. Quick,
Give me the password, or I shall arrest you.

KÖNIGSMARK.
Back knave! your hand is on a gentleman.

BAUMAIN.
I'll prove my title to as good a name,
If you resist me. (*Draws.*)

KÖNIGSMARK.
    Are you drunk, you clown,
To take death's tools for playthings? Sheathe your
 sword!
You are too nimble with your rapier,
To know its proper use.

BAUMAIN.
      Come, teach me then.
Your backward fashion shames my nimbleness.

KÖNIGSMARK.
Why, what word-valiant roysterer are you
Who quarrel with my kindness? Walk with me
Into the courtyard, and, mayhap, I'll give
Your valor a short breathing. In the palace,
'Tis treason to draw swords. You call yourself
A guard on duty; but I doubt your words;
For, to my knowledge, you are the first man
Who e'er stood sentry here.

BAUMAIN.
     Will you not yield?

KÖNIGSMARK.
I am Count Königsmark, your Colonel, man;
Will that suffice?

BAUMAIN.

I know you not, I say.

Sir, I arrest you.

KÖNIGSMARK.

Show your warrant then,
And I will follow you.

BAUMAIN.

My warrant's out—
Here, in my hand—warrant and power enough
To take a score of such gallants as you.

KÖNIGSMARK.

You saucy knave, give way and let me pass,
Or I shall lose my patience.

BAUMAIN.

By the saints.
If words were feats, I'd run away for fear!
You pass not here, sir. Either you must yield,
Or I must take you.

KÖNIGSMARK.

Yield myself to you,
A vaporing, drunken braggart, with no right,
Nor form of warrant, to arrest my steps!
Look you; my way lies yonder, through that door;
Move hand or foot to stay me, and I'll whip
Your carcass to a jelly!—Step aside!
I would not draw my sword upon such game.

BAUMAIN.

Stand back! you walk upon my weapon's point:
The next step will be fatal.

KÖNIGSMARK.

     Stubborn fool!
Are you so desperate? Make way, or, by Heaven,
I'll make way through you! (*Draws.*)

(*They fight.* KÖNIGSMARK *drives* BAUMAIN.)

BAUMAIN.

    Help, help!—treason!—help!

KÖNIGSMARK.

Poor coward!—

(*Enter Guards, who strike down* KÖNIGSMARK.)

BAUMAIN.

   Hold! you shall not mangle him.

FIRST GUARD.

Oh, look! it is our Colonel!

SECOND GUARD.

     What, the Count?

BAUMAIN.

I'll hang you all, without an hour of grace,
If by mischance this story get abroad.

THIRD GUARD.

I'd rather have seen Hans, my brother, there,
With all those gashes, in that pool of blood,
Than him who lies there.

SECOND GUARD.

     Is he dead?

FIRST GUARD.

        Stone dead.
I struck a blow across his shoulder, Paul,
That would have slain Goliah.

SECOND GUARD.

        How he bleeds!

FIRST GUARD.

God curse the hand that did it!

BAUMAIN.

        Come away!
What are you muttering there? Go in, you knaves!
He was a traitor.

FIRST GUARD.

     If he was, I'd like
To find a loyal man in Hanover.
        [*Exeunt Guards.*

BAUMAIN.

They take it hard; and I myself would choose
Some kinder duty, if I were my own.
Poor Königsmark! There lies the boldest heart
That ever led a soldier through a breach.

(*Re-enter* COUNTESS VON PLATEN.)

COUNTESS VON PLATEN.

Is it all over?

BAUMAIN.

   Yes.

COUNTESS VON PLATEN.

     You made a noise.

BAUMAIN.
Not much.

COUNTESS VON PLATEN.
Too much. He's dead?

BAUMAIN.
I think so, Countess:
He has not moved.

COUNTESS VON PLATEN.
I'm sorry he is dead;
For I had something I would say to him.

BAUMAIN.
Say to him now!

COUNTESS VON PLATEN.
Yes, now. Withdraw a space;
But do not go too far. Remain in sight;
And leave your flambeau with me.
[*Exit* BAUMAIN.
His heart beats;
The angry color has not died away
From his warm brow. How noble he appears,
Stretched like a hero on an ancient tomb!
Philip, awake! Oh, how I loved this man!
She stole him from me. Heart, heart, will you beat
Ever again for your Sophia? No!
The hand which I have laid upon his fate
Makes him my own for ever.

KÖNIGSMARK.
O kind Heaven,
Let me not perish!

COUNTESS VON PLATEN.
                Philip Königsmark,
You know me?

KÖNIGSMARK.
        Yes; you are Elizabeth,
A lady I have injured; and I beg
To be forgiven.

COUNTESS VON PLATEN.
        Hush, hush! You'll fill my life
With horrors, and my dreams with hell itself.
Curse me—forgive not—I beseech you, curse!
Know you who did this deed?

KÖNIGSMARK.
                Some brutal tools
Of the Elector or Prince George.

COUNTESS VON PLATEN.
                        No, no;
I did it.

KÖNIGSMARK.
    You? Then God forgive you!—oh!

COUNTESS VON PLATEN.
You suffer much?

KÖNIGSMARK.
        Yes, yes; but, at my heart,
I suffer more for all concerned in this,
And most for you. Your feet are in my blood—
Your skirts are fringed with it—your hands are red:
Where'er you walk, that track shall follow you,—
A stream of crimson through the shuddering day,

A trail of fire by night. Unhappy wretch,
You shall not dare to look behind, for fear
Of your own footsteps; and where'er you pause,
This pool of blood shall form around your feet,
Like a foul sorcerer's circle; while, before,
Hope shall be dead, and memory, behind,
Shall lash you like a fury! Pray to die.

COUNTESS VON PLATEN.

Oh! mercy, mercy!

KÖNIGSMARK.

      Take your hands away
From your white face! your hands are purple too,—
Stained to the bone with the infernal dye.

COUNTESS VON PLATEN.

Oh, Philip, spare me! I have murdered you
From love, not hatred—jealousy and love
Blinded my sight.—I do not hate you now:
I'd give my life to save you, if with life,
Your love for me returned.

KÖNIGSMARK.

      I loathe you, woman,
As Heaven commands us to loathe wickedness.
I wish no harm to you: I would not move
A finger to revenge myself. Ah, no;
I leave you to Heaven's justice,—the complete,
Full, even justice of far-sighted Heaven.
What more could I desire, for my revenge,
Than God will give you? Quit me; let me die
In peace; your presence troubles me. You seem
An evil thought, thrust between me and Heaven.

If you are aught but pure and total fiend,
Grant my last prayer. It will not try you much,
To keep the pledge, when I am in my grave.

COUNTESS VON PLATEN.

What is it?

KÖNIGSMARK.

Spare the Princess.

COUNTESS VON PLATEN.

Villain, peace!
You dare to love her yet? She brought you here;
This was her doing: I, a poor blind tool,
Driven by her poisonous sweetness here and there,
Struck wildly in the dark, I knew not what;
And so I slew you.

KÖNIGSMARK.

Murderous sophistry!
The devil has a salve for every sin:
You are all devil.—Go, go!

COUNTESS VON PLATEN.

Königsmark,
I see her coming; I am going hence;
And in the dark she'll stumble over you.

KÖNIGSMARK.

Fiend, fiend!

COUNTESS VON PLATEN.

I see it now; she wears her cloak,
Her traveling clothes, a parcel's in her hand!—
Ha, ha! I understand; you would elope—

To-night you two would flee together, ha!
Get up, and follow her—ha, ha! I think
I balked your project! When I come again,
You'll see me spare the Princess!
[Exit with torch.

KÖNIGSMARK.

Has the earth
Patience to bear this monster on its breast!

(*Enter* SOPHIA *with* COUNTESS VON KNESEBECK, *carrying a light.*)

SOPHIA.

How dark it is! I almost fear to cross
This dismal hall. But are you very sure
The horses are in waiting?—Hush! what's that?

COUNTESS VON KNESEBECK.

I heard no sound.

SOPHIA.

I did,—a breathing. Hark!
Heaven's mercy! what is here? A bleeding man—
A murdered man!—Philip!

COUNTESS VON KNESEBECK.

Oh! terrible!

KÖNIGSMARK.

Yes, Princess, dying, but by hard degrees.

SOPHIA.

Fly, Countess! bring some napkins, and the flask
That sits upon my table. Stand not there,

Staring in helpless horror! fly, fly, fly!
He's dying—oh, my God, he's dying!
[*Exit* COUNTESS VON KNESEBECK.

KÖNIGSMARK.

       Yes;
But sweetly now. What bliss it were to die,
As I lie thus! Oh take me, Heaven, I pray!
Receive me from her pure, religious hands;
Prize the poor offering for the donor's sake,
And overlook my gross defects! Alas!
I am selfish in my happiness. Away!
You wait your ruin, if you tarry here!

SOPHIA.

Who used you thus?

KÖNIGSMARK.

    The Countess, our old foe.
She had the hardihood to boast of it,
And hiss her malice in my dying ears.
She left me, as you came, with furious threats
Against you, Princess. She will soon return,
To consummate her vengeance. Leave me! Flee!
And save yourself!

SOPHIA.

    I will not, dare not go.
God's eye is on me, Philip: what will he
Say to the wretch who leaves a dying friend,
To seek her safety?

KÖNIGSMARK.

                I implore you, flee!
Your presence makes me wretched. I shall die
With greater comfort for your absence.—Go!

SOPHIA.

I will not go! I claim a higher right—
A right you'll not deny me. Listen, then;
I love you, Philip: not as you, perhaps,
Would have me love, but, oh, as tenderly,
As deeply and as firmly. To my heart
You were a brother: when my lips said " Philip,"
My heart meant brother. Shall I quit you now—
Leave my dear brother dying in the dark—
Skulk like a coward from a fancied fear?
The thought is odious. Were the world agape,
And all its sneering faces fixed on me,
Here would I kneel beside you. Ah, poor heart!
How helpless love folds up his soaring plumes
Beneath the shadow of death's awful wings!
Save him, just Heaven!—he is too bright a soul—
We cannot spare him—save him, gentle Heaven!

KÖNIGSMARK.

You love me as a sister. To my thoughts,
Made cold and pure by death's allaying hand,
That love seems better than the senses' heat,
And fitter for the realm to which I go.
Do not forget it in this world of yours,
Among its cares and changes. I shall wait—
I know not where—but I shall wait for you,—
A pining soul that cannot turn towards heaven
For earthly bondage.

SOPHIA.

    Philip, you are faint.—
Faint, said I, faint? Oh, mercy! those dull eyes
That wander through the air, and nowhere rest,
Those sharpening features, and that gurgling breath,
Tell fearful tidings. Do not leave me yet!
Stretch life a little, wave destruction back,
And tarry here a moment!

(*Re-enter* COUNTESS VON KNESEBECK.)

KÖNIGSMARK.

    It is vain.—
Yet will I stay for this.

(*Enter the* ELECTOR, COUNTESS VON PLATEN, BAUMAIN, *Guards, Attendants, etc., with torches, etc.*)

COUNTESS VON PLATEN.

    See, see, your Grace!
She wears her traveling clothes. Need I say more?
Your eyes find argument in all they see.
Elopement was her aim. She and the Count
Would have been leagues away, before this time,
Had I not interposed.

KÖNIGSMARK.

  'Tis false—all false!

SOPHIA.

Dare you, with murder fresh upon your soul,
Pile crime on crime? Is God immovable?
Is lightning harmless? and is thunder dumb?

Look here, assassin, at your bloody work,—
At this majestic evidence of heaven,
Torn into shreds by your unholy hands!
You dare not. Think you that the end is here?
No, with the high commission of the Lord,
I tell you, woman, in a prophet's voice,
This deed frowns on you from eternity,
And gathers terrors from the rolling years!

ELECTOR.

Most mournful sight!

COUNTESS VON PLATEN.
       Ernest, be resolute.

SOPHIA.

Peace! he would speak.

KÖNIGSMARK.
       Your Highness, hark to me.
I am dying, as you see; I lie almost
Within the outer judgment-court of heaven,
Nearer by leagues than you who stand around:
Falsehood cannot avail me. Hear me swear,
Standing before the awful bar of sin,
That, even in thought, the Princess is as pure
As the white dove that breasts the silver morn
In her first flight. I swear it, o'er and o'er!

COUNTESS VON PLATEN.

Could he say less?

SOPHIA.

          O vile interpreter
Of a fair text!

ELECTOR.

     Remove the Princess hence.
At fitting time, her case shall have my care,

    (*Guards seize* SOPHIA.)

SOPHIA.

Unhand me, ruffians! I will not be forced
To quit my duty. He has paused a while—
My more than brother, my one, only friend—
Upon the treacherous outworks of the world,
To say farewell. I will not go till he
Has closed his eyes, and given me leave to go.

COUNTESS VON PLATEN.

Hark, Ernest, hark!

ELECTOR.

      I hear. Away with her!

SOPHIA.

Cruel villains, are you merciless? Your Grace,
Grant me one moment—but a little while!
See how his spirit rushes to its end!
Philip—dear Philip!

    (*Guards drag her off.*)

KÖNIGSMARK.

   (*Starting up.*) She is innocent—
Oh, spare the Princess—she is innocent! (*Falls.*)

BAUMAIN.

Madam, Count Königsmark is dead.

COUNTESS VON PLATEN.

Dead—dead! (*Faints.*)

THE LEGEND OF THE HOUNDS.

THE LEGEND OF THE HOUNDS.

COLEBROOK FURNACE in Cornwall stands,
Crouched at the foot of the iron lands,—
The wondrous hill of iron ore
That pours its wealth through the furnace-door,
Is mixed with lime and smothered in wood,
Tortured with fire till a molten flood
Leaps from the taps to the sow below
And her littered pigs that round her glow:
So that a gazer, looking down
The moulding floor from the platform's crown,
Might think, if fancy helped the spell,
He saw a grate in the roof of hell.
Around the furnace, far and near,
Slag and cinder spread year by year.
Never a blade of grass or flower
Stood in the sun or bowed in the shower;
Never a robin whistled nigh,
Or a swallow clove the grimy sky;
No cattle browsed, or musing stood
A summer's noon in the acrid flood:
Cursed and cursing, a thing of hate,
In its waste the moody furnace sate,

And the loathful breezes slowly led
The reek away from its flickering head,
To shower the poison down again
On arid hill and blighted plain.

Howbeit, this devil's labor rolled
Back on the Squire in floods of gold.
Gold and hunting and potent drink,
And loud-tongued girls, that grin and wink
Over the flagon's dripping brim,
These were the things that busied him.
Strong of sinew and dull of mind,
He blustered round like a winter wind.
You could hear his laugh come on before
While his hounds were off a mile or more;
And in the wassail he stormed and roared,
Clashing his fist on the groaning board,
Or clutched his trulls till their young bones bent,
And they shrieked at his savage merriment.
No being called the ruffian friend;
Gold was his all; the power to lend
Bought service of the groveling fear
Which fawns, because it dares not sneer,
And there it ended. Save the beasts
Who guzzled with him at his feasts,
Or, worse, the wantons whose caress
Was sold, he was companionless
Of man or woman. One rare hound,
The wonder of the country round—
Flora, the leader of his pack—
Followed, a shadow, in his track;—
Followed despite his kicks and blows,
Paused when he paused, rose when he rose;

THE LEGEND OF THE HOUNDS.

Nestled between his clumsy feet
When all the table swam with heat,
And causeless oath and witless joke
Around the swinish circle broke;
And sometimes when her drunken lord
Slid stupefied beneath the board,
And stouter comrades jeered his plight,
With pointed thumbs and laughter light,
She howled above the Squire's disgrace,
Or, moaning, licked his flaming face.
In field no hound could hold the scent
With Flora, as she bounding went
Ten lengths before the yelping chase,
And kept throughout her leading place.
No hound, however great of pride,
Had ever reached her milk-white side;
Unchallenged in the flying front,
She shone, a star, to all the hunt.
To this fair brute the selfish Squire
Showed favor sometimes, sometimes ire.
Upon her head he smote his spite;
Or when his sluggish heart was light,
He soothed her forehead, pulled her ear,
Or tossed her morsels from his cheer.
But cuff or kindness could not move
The temper of her steadfast love.
Serene, unfearing, taking all
That his capricious hand let fall,
Whether it smoothed or bruised a limb,
As grace, so it but came from him.
No moment passed, by day or night,
That Flora held him not in sight;

And haply when his business took
The Squire from home, her haggard look,
Her anxious whine and listening ear,
Her busy snufflings far and near,
Her almost meaning human talk,
As his great boots ground up the walk;
The yelp, the burst of boundless love
With which she crawled to him, and clove
Close to his side, whate'er his mood,
Shamed the best passion of our blood.

One winter night when half the world
Was drowned in snow, whose billows curled
Above all landmarks—when the breeze
Stung, like a swarm of angry bees,
And made the traveler wild and blind—
The Squire, half-drunken, left behind
Some neighboring revelers, to essay
Across the fields his homeward way.
How long he wandered, why or how
He reached the mountain's highest brow,
Straggling unheedful a stone's cast
From his own pale, and onward passed
Across the road and frozen brook,
While his chilled muscles crept and shook,
And each strong spasm of the gust
Half-smothered him with snowy dust—
Was that which from his torpid state
His memory could not separate.
At last, bewildered at his plight,
He laughed; and with a spirit light,
Because the snow was soft and deep,
Thought he would rest himself in sleep.

He was not cold now nor afraid;
"For daylight will soon break," he said.
And the last things that crossed his mind,
Ere his numb senses he resigned
To sleep, was snow, snow, snow all round,
And the far baying of a hound.

Flora throughout the night had been
In grievous trouble, and her mien
Struck all the servants. O'er and o'er
She scratched and whimpered at the door,
Begging to pass, though still denied
Because the storm so raged outside.
At length, despairing of the Squire,
The house made ready to retire;—
"For surely no one, in his mind,
Would brave this awful snow and wind;"—
When suddenly from off her lair,
With ears erect, with every hair
Bristling upon her snowy hide,
Jaw hanging, eyes distended wide,
Tail rigid, twitching lip and nose,
Flora amidst the servants rose.
Paused in the middle of a bound,
Like silence listening for a sound,—
Paused but one moment. With a cry,
Or scream, said they then standing by,
Sheer through the glass she drove her way
Into the night. Oh such a bay—
So clear, so clarion-like, so shrill—
Never arose on Cornwall hill,
When the spent fox toiled full in view,
And Flora heard the Squire's halloo,

As through the powdered snow she tore,
With nothing visible before,
With nothing but God's hand to trace
The rout and purpose of her chase!
She reached the Squire, a rigid heap;
Already the thick, fatal sleep
Was heavy on him; and the snow
Was rising, like a tidal flow,
Around his person. Brow and beard
Were buried quite, as Flora reared
Her form above him. So she stood
An instant in a thoughtful mood;
Then barked, bayed, bellowed in his ear,
Mad with the passion of her fear;
Licked his stiff nostrils and his cheek,
Mouthed the dull lips that could not speak;
Tugged at his garments, fiercely tore
His listless hands until the gore
Ran trickling slowly; and at length,
With all the vigor of her strength,
Dragged him along, good half a rood;
And fairly on his feet she stood
The man, bewildered and half dead,
Who staggered forward where she led,
With her long muzzle holding tight
His outer coat; and then a light—
He knew not when—he could not say—
Flashed round him, like a sudden day;
And somehow, stumbling. so he fell
Across his threshold—who could tell!—
Bursting apart the shattered door.
Long after that, he knew no more

Until he wakened in his bed,
With Flora resting her white head
Between his knees, and her soft eyes
Fixed on his own, serenely wise.

But all this happened long ago;
And many a storm of windy snow
Had capped the hill and filled the dell,
Since Flora's chase was news to tell.
A calm that scarcely made the trees
Nod recognition to the breeze
That from the south came up, and died
Along the tawny mountain-side;
A dull, warm day, all cloud and haze;
As hunters know, the day of days
For sport behind the vocal pack,
Once fastened on the fox's track.—
Such was the favored day that bent
Above the Squire, as forth he went,
Noisy and boastful, as of old,
To show some city friends how bold
His horses were before a fence;
And how the depths of every sense
Were stirred when all the hounds gave tongue,
And down the hills the whole hunt swung,
With whoop and halloo, bark and bay,
And o'er the country scoured away.
"I'll show them—by the Lord!—I'll show
Such scenes as cockneys never know,
Prowling about their filthy streets,
Where plague at every window beats,
And Nature, like a beggar pale,
Stares vaguely through a grass-plot rail!"

His vulgar burst of pride indeed
But gave the Cornwall lands their meed.
It seemed as though the fields and skies
Had interchanged their wonted dies;
So dark the clouds, so bright the wood,
Glazed over with a dewy flood.
Purple and gold and flaming sheen
Stood out against the evergreen
That, here and there, in clumps and spires,
Defied October's painted fires;
And far away with mighty swell,
Like a great pillar thrust from hell,
The fumes of Colebrook Furnace stood
In dismal weight above the wood.

For all his boasts, the Squire's fine pack
Sulked at the outset, and held back,
With drooping tail and humble head,
And deprecating eyes that said,
Almost as tongues, this morning's sport
Finds us with spirits slack and short.
The Huntsman and the angry Whips,
With curses hissing through their lips,
Drove the reluctant dogs along,
A sullen and rebellious throng.
Flora herself had lost her pride,
And strayed, with vacant eyes, mouth wide
And lolling tongue, behind them all,
Deaf to her duty's urgent call.
In wrath the Squire exclaimed, "Why, zounds!
Matthew, what ails these cursed hounds?"
"I know not, sir," replied the Whip,
"Unless some scoundrel chose to slip

A drug into their feed last night,
To do your promises a spite.
These city chaps—" "Pshaw! drive along!
And—damn your mercy!—use the thong!"
"No good in that. We'd best turn back.
You'll get no run, Squire, from the pack.
And see yon cockney's tallow face;
He's grinning at our hounds' disgrace!"
Across the Squire's low brow a band
Of crimson came. His strong right hand
Closed on his whip-stock till the thorn
Cracked in his clutch. A growl of scorn
Rolled from his lips, to see the smile
Flitting around him. For a while
He paused in doubt, then cried, "Away,
To covert! Give the dogs fair play!
And if they fail us there, why then—
But give the pack a chance, my men!"
Into the brush the Huntsman led,
Shaking his doubting grizzled head;
And the keen Whips, on either side,
Flanked the dull pack, and closely pried
Hither and thither; till—oh shame
To them and to the pack's wide fame!—
Before their startled eyes they saw
Sly reynard from the covert draw,
With brush in air, and skurry by,
Without a tongue to make reply
To the rogue's challenge. "There, look there!
A fox, by Satan! And I swear,
If I have eyes, the rascal rose
Almost beneath white Flora's nose!

Drive out the curs! Is this the way
You beat a covert? Out, I say!"
The devilish temper of the Squire
Burst outward; as a furious fire,
That long has gnawed a roof, at last
Breaks through it with a sudden blast,
And leaps revealed, and towers on high
In flames and sparks against the sky.
Amid the cowering dogs he dashed,
Rode over some, cursed all, and lashed
Even Flora till her milky side
With trickling crimson welts was dyed.
He raved and punished while his arm
Had strength to do the smallest harm;
Then paused, with flaming eyes, white lips,
And bellowed at the trembling Whips:
"Drive out, you scoundrels!" "Drive, sir?—
    where?"—
Just then the misty autumn air
Looked darker for a heavy smoke
That, rolling from the Furnace, broke
Above the woods, and waved its plume
Portentous of a coming doom.
"Where? Why to Colebrook, down the glen.
I'll show these town-bred gentlemen,
If my dogs cannot hunt so well
On earth, another hunt in hell!"
Bawled the mad Squire; and all the beast
In his base nature so increased,
That he could crown the deed he sought
With laughter brutal as the thought.
So the whole hunt towards Colebrook rode,
Marveling at what the Squire forbode

By those strange words. Across the waste
Of slag and cinder slowly paced
The snorting steeds; and hanging back,
Whipped to each step, the drooping pack
Followed perforce. Ah! well I know
That some foul malice of a foe
Had practiced on the noble hound;
Or what that day could so confound
Great nature's instinct, and so shame
The faithful creature's well-won fame?
Beside the Furnace, wondering still
What freak the angry Squire might will,
The hunt dismounted. "Up!" he said,
"Up with you, to the furnace-head!
Yes, bring the dogs." The Whips looked blank.
Some muttered, "Nonsense!" and some shrank
From the fierce heat that overran
The reeking walls. "Up, dog and man!"
Yelled forth the Squire. "By Heaven, you'll rue,
If any balk the thing I'd do!"
That they knew well: so up they sped,
Still grumbling, to the furnace-head.
"Call here the firemen!" And they came,
Grimy with dust, those sons of flame,
Half-brute, scarce human, drudges base,
Bound to their mean and groveling place
By natures not a whit above
The abject work at which they strove.
Beneath them, panting, rose and fell
The surface of that pot of hell.
Great logs of wood, and limestone gray,
And tons of ore, all boiled away

In one huge mass, that seethed and fumed,
Crackled and sparkled, flashed and gloomed,
And belched its sulphurous breath around,
Reeking aloft towards heaven's profound:
As though the devil's self had planned
A cunning engine, reared and manned,
Once more to wage against the Lord
The battle lost him by the sword.
A hundred curious eyes exchanged
Looks with their neighbors, as they ranged—
Hunters and firemen, and the crew
Of idlers who the chase pursue—
Around the dreadful caldron's jaws,
Waiting the Squire's behest. A pause—
In which the crackling of the coals,
The sobbing vapor, and the rolls
Of pitchy smoke seemed strangely clear—
Fell on the gazer's eye and ear.
Then spoke the Squire; and if his breath
Had flamed like that vast pit of death,
Wilder dismay would not have hung
Upon the mandate of his tongue.
"Come here, you drones, and work a spell!
Look to your furnace! Can you tell
What needs a fire so dull and slack?
Feed it, you sluggards, with this pack!"
A cry, or protest rather, rose
From every lip before the close
Of those infernal words. Thank Heaven,
'Twas echoed by the lowest even!
Thank God, in man's behalf, I can
Record it for the sake of man!

Back from the furnace reeled the throng,
Stung to the heart; but stern and strong
As the dark, pitiless, vague form
That reigns in Hades, when the storm
Of wrath is wildest, and the lost
On blazing waves are upward tossed,
Pale with their tortures; so the Squire,
Grim and unshaken in his ire,
With deadly calmness slowly said,
"Do as I order!" White with dread,
That beautified their dusky clay,
The dolts, who dared not disobey,
Approached the hounds. Oh, wonder not
At the poor serfs; for on that spot,
Such was their master's power and awe
That his mere nod was more than law;
'Twas fate, 'twas sustenance to come
To them and to the mouths at home.

Into the flames with howl and yell,
Hurled by the rugged firemen, fell
That pack of forty. Better hounds,
Fuller of music, of the sounds
That fire the hunter, drawing near
His furry prey with whoop and cheer—
The dogs all bursting in full cry,
Crashing through brush and timber high—
Never could Cornwall boast; and still
The silent lands lament their ill,
And the mysterious spell that lay
Upon them on that fatal day.
For now the bubbling liquid fire
Swallowed them all. Beside the Squire,

Flora alone stood desolate,
Sole relique of the general fate.
A hundred times had Flora dashed,
As some poor comrade yelling plashed
Into the sparkling molten lake,
With cries that any heart might shake—
A hundred times had Flora sprung,
Half frantic, moaning, giving tongue,
Up to the very furnace-brim,
Then slowly backward crawled to him,
Her lord, her idol, with her eyes
Speaking her piteous surprise.
"What, you vile wanton, are you there?
In with the bitch!" "But, Squire—" "I swear
I'll brain the fool that wags a lip!"
Up rose his heavy hunting-whip:
Another word had sent it full
Upon the talker's naked skull.
"In with her! She's the last and worst:
Mere justice should have sent her first!"
Towards her approached the loathful gang;
But Flora bared her ivory fang,
And snarled a warning. Every hair
That bristled on her said—"Beware!"
As crouching low, her dangerous eye
Fixed on the ruffians drawing nigh,
She fairly awed them, till they stood
Quailing before her lion mood.
"You shrinking cowards!" foamed the Squire,
Now with redoubled rage afire,
"Is't for your pretty skins you fear
To venture? Flora!—here, dog, here!"

At once the look of wrath was gone;
A trusting, tender, loving dawn
Rose in her eyes; her talking tail
Quivered with joy; a low, soft wail
Broke from her, as the iron hand
Of the stout Squire from off her stand
Swung her; and striding towards the ledge
With his pleased burden, on the edge
Of awful death—oh, foul disgrace!—
She turned and licked his purple face.
Sheer out he flung her. As she fell,
Up from that palpitating hell
Came three shrill cries, and then a roll
Of thunder. Every pallid soul
Shrank from the pit; and ghastly white,
As was the snow one winter night,
The Squire reeled backward. Long he gazed
From face to face; then asked, amazed,
"Was it a fancy? If you heard,
Answer! What was it?—that last word
Which Flora flung me?" Answer came,
As though one mouth pronounced the name,
And smote the asker as a rod;
"The word she said was—'God, God, God!'"

Home rode the Squire with heavy mind.
Why did he turn and look behind
So often, seeming there to trace
Something that followed pace by pace?
What was the meaning of his sighs,
His wistful looks in other's eyes,
As though he wished to solve a doubt
Of that he dared not ask about?

Why was he so bewildered?—so
Astray in talking? Where the flow
Of those coarse spirits that so long
Had buoyed him up through sin and wrong?
What was it? Something was not right
About him; that was plain to sight.

After that hunt, a change began
To work upon the stricken man.
Sulky and dismal, still and shy,
He skulked to shun the public eye.
Comrade by comrade gave him up.
No more for him the festal cup
Went round; no more the drunken jeer
Through peals of laughter smote the ear.
His table spread its leaves no more
To tempt his cronies to his door.
The girls, he one time loved so well,
Shrank from the strange abiding spell
That lay upon him. All alone
With some dread secret of his own,
That shook him with a nervous fear
When man or maid or child drew near—
Some mystery that shunned the light,
And stole away from common sight,
Burdened his mind, and made his ways
Sad to behold—he passed his days.
Hour after hour, with listless air,
He'd idly rock upon his chair;
But this strange fact was marked by all,
Who served his sullen beck and call,
That ever, as he took his seat,
It seemed as though his shrinking feet

Were pushed apart by something, seen
But by himself. As strange his mien
In walking; for his hanging hand
He'd often snatch, as though a brand
Were laid against it. Often, too,
When his house-door he entered through,
He'd slam it tight, as though he tried
To shut upon the outer side
Some odious follower. Of the Squire
But this remained, a thirst like fire
For drink, drink ever. Tawny wine,
Or the pale vintage of the Rhine,
Or crimson claret, or the cup
That foams and sparkles, he gave up
For that accursed fiend whose eye
Glares through the spirit of the rye,
And scatters o'er this hapless land
Wreck, woe and death on every hand.
From morn till eve, the whisky ran
In burning torrents through the man ;
And often in the middle night,
Or when the sky was gray with light,
The waking servants heard the clink
Of glass, forerunning drink, more drink.

The Squire's bad way of life at length
Told even on his rugged strength :
The drink gnawed slowly to the seat
Of life itself. His tottering feet,
His moist, dull eyes, his mottled skin,
The stupor deadening all within,
The silly giggle, and the wink
With which he clutched the fatal drink—

All these things said to any ear,
The Squire's last hour is drawing near:
Cut out the cloth, and wax the thread,
To make a garment for the dead!
Twice spasms had seized him; fancies dread
Of snakes and vermin thronged his bed.
Male nurses, from the distant town,
Between his gnashing teeth forced down
Strong opiates; while his wakeful eyes
Flared here and there, with vague surprise,
At visions which he tried to touch
With care, their seeming truth was such.
Slowly he rallied from these spells,
Emerging from long sleep; and hell's
Apparent purpose twice was foiled.
So the poor mortal slowly toiled
Back into life; and for a tide
He and the draught of suicide
Were strangers; but some influence,
That had the mastery of his sense,
Would draw him down, till once again
The demon held his deadly reign.

For the third time at length he lay
Upon his bed. The heat and fray,
The feverous phantoms all were gone;
And sane in mind, but most forlorn,
He panted onward through the dark;
Drifting along like some wrecked bark,
Blown inward towards a misty coast,
That shouts with all its white-capped host,
From every bar and headland near,
A warning which Fate laughs to hear.

He spoke: "Where's Flora?" None replied.
"That's strange!" and then he weakly tried
To peer around. "Gone, gone! then I
Must follow!" With a dreary sigh,
As one accepts a coming fate,
Foredoomed him from the earliest date,
The Squire turned slowly on his bed.
"Open the curtains; raise my head!
For I must look my last to-night
On Colebrook Furnace. What a light
Circles its head! What angry reeks,
In blue and white and yellow streaks,
Roll o'er it, flashing high and higher,
Whene'er they feed the raging fire!
Give me some drink.—Not that damned stuff,
But whisky! I have had enough
Of doctors' potions. Let me slip,
With honest liquor on my lip,
Out of this life. I long to flee:
Better may come; worse cannot be."
As he was ordered thus, the nurse
Held long and oft the liquid curse
To the Squire's mouth. The leech had said,
Shaking his placid smiling head,
"When the spent wretch rejects his draught"—
And here the fawning nurse had laughed—
"His hour will be at hand." The Squire
Gazed long on Colebrook's lurid fire.
A while he muttered to himself
Of dogs and horses, girls and pelf;
Or softer fancies of the child
Made pictures, till he almost smiled.

But suddenly, with fearful cries,
Through the wide sash he fixed his eyes;
Then strained, and rose, full half his length,
Upon his mattress, by main strength,
Shouting, so all the house might hear,
Aghast with more than mortal fear,—
"Here they all come, the hellish pack,
Pouring from Colebrook Furnace, back
Into the world! Oh, see, see, see!
They snuff, to get the wind of me!
They've found it! Flora heads the whole,—
Whiter than any snows that roll
O'er Cornwall's hills, and bury deep
The wanderer in blissful sleep.
Ho! mark them! We shall have a run
Before this ghastly meet is done!
Now they give tongue! They've found their prey!
Here they come crashing—all this way—
And all afire! And it is I—
Weak as I am, and like to die—
Who must be hunted!" With a bound
He reached the floor, and fled around;
Once, twice, thrice, round the room he fled,
Then in the nurse's arms fell dead.

Still Colebrook Furnace grimly stands,
Waving its plume o'er Cornwall's lands,
Blighting the air with poisoned breath,
Spreading its bounds of waste and death,
Its slag and cinder, dry and dun,
That nothing green will grow upon;
Still, like a hoary king, it rears
Its head among its dismal peers;

Still at its glowing feet are rolled
The floods that turn to wicked gold;
Still beasts, birds, reptiles shun the place,
And man alone will do it grace;
The Squire and all his race are gone;
But this wild legend still lives on.
Christ save us from the wretched fate
Of him who dared his wrath to sate
On God's dumb creatures, as of old
Befell the Squire of whom I told!

MISCELLANEOUS POEMS.

COUNTESS LAURA.

IT was a dreary day in Padua,
   The Countess Laura, for a single year
Fernando's wife, upon her bridal bed,
Like an uprooted lily on the snow,
The withered outcast of a festival,
Lay dead. She died of some uncertain ill,
That struck her almost on her wedding-day,
And clung to her, and dragged her slowly down,
Thinning her cheeks and pinching her full lips,
Till, in her chance, it seemed that with a year
Full half a century was overpast.
In vain had Paracelsus taxed his art,
And feigned a knowledge of her malady;
In vain had all the doctors, far and near,
Gathered around the mystery of her bed,
Draining her veins, her husband's treasury,
And physic's jargon, in a fruitless quest
For causes equal to the dread result.
The Countess only smiled when they were gone,
Hugged her fair body with her little hands,
And turned upon her pillows wearily,
As though she fain would sleep, no common sleep,
But the long, breathless slumber of the grave.
She hinted nothing. Feeble as she was,
The rack could not have wrung her secret out.
The Bishop, when he shrived her, coming forth,

Cried, in a voice of heavenly ecstasy,
"O blessed soul! with nothing to confess,
Save virtues and good deeds, which she mistakes—
So humble is she—for our human sins!"
Praying for death, she tossed upon her bed,
Day after day; as might a shipwrecked bark
That rocks upon one billow, and can make
No onward motion towards her port of hope.
At length, one morn, when those around her said,
"Surely the Countess mends, so fresh a light
Beams from her eyes and beautifies her face,"—
One morn in spring, when every flower of earth
Was opening to the sun, and breathing up
Its votive incense, her impatient soul
Opened itself, and so exhaled to heaven.
When the Count heard it, he reeled back a pace;
Then turned with anger on the messenger;
Then craved his pardon, and wept out his heart
Before the menial; tears, ah me! such tears
As love sheds only, and love only once.
Then he bethought him, "Shall this wonder die,
And leave behind no shadow? not a trace
Of all the glory that environed her,
That mellow nimbus circling round my star?"
So, with his sorrow glooming in his face,
He paced along his gallery of Art,
And strode among the painters, where they stood,
With Carlo, the Venetian, at their head,
Studying the Masters by the dawning light
Of his transcendent genius. Through the groups
Of gayly-vestured artists moved the Count;
As some lone cloud of thick and leaden hue,
Packed with the secret of a coming storm,

Moves through the gold and crimson evening
    mists,
Deadening their splendor. In a moment, still
Was Carlo's voice, and still the prattling crowd;
And a great shadow overwhelmed them all,
As their white faces and their anxious eyes
Pursued Fernando in his moody walk.
He paused, as one who balances a doubt,
Weighing two courses, then burst out with this:
"Ye all have seen the tidings in my face;
Or has the dial ceased to register
The workings of my heart? Then hear the bell,
That almost cracks its frame in utterance;
The Countess—she is dead!"—"Dead!" Carlo
    groaned.
And if a bolt from middle heaven had struck
His splendid features full upon the brow,
He could not have appeared more scathed and
    blanched.
"Dead!—dead!" He staggered to his easel-frame,
And clung around it, buffeting the air
With one wild arm, as though a drowning man
Hung to a spar and fought against the waves.
The Count resumed: "I came not here to grieve,
Nor see my sorrow in another's eyes.
Who'll paint the Countess, as she lies to-night
In state within the chapel? Shall it be
That earth must lose her wholly? that no hint
Of her gold tresses, beaming eyes, and lips
That talked in silence, and the eager soul
That ever seemed outbreaking through her clay,
And scattering glory round it,—shall all these
Be dull corruption's heritage, and we,

Poor beggars, have no legacy to show
That love she bore us? That were shame to love,
And shame to you, my masters." Carlo stalked
Forth from his easel, stiffly as a thing
Moved by mechanic impulse. His thin lips,
And sharpened nostrils, and wan, sunken cheeks,
And the cold glimmer in his dusky eyes,
Made him a ghastly sight. The throng drew back,
As though they let a spectre through. Then he,
Fronting the Count, and speaking in a voice
Sounding remote and hollow, made reply:
"Count, I shall paint the Countess. 'Tis my fate,—
Not pleasure,—no, nor duty." But the Count,
Astray in woe, but understood assent,
Not the strange words that bore it; and he flung
His arm round Carlo, drew him to his breast,
And kissed his forehead. At which Carlo shrank:
Perhaps 'twas at the honor. Then the Count,
A little reddening at his public state,—
Unseemly to his near and recent loss,—
Withdrew in haste between the downcast eyes
That did him reverence as he rustled by.

Night fell on Padua. In the chapel lay
The Countess Laura at the altar's foot.
Her coronet glittered on her pallid brows;
A crimson pall, weighed down with golden work,
Sown thick with pearls, and heaped with early
    flowers,
Draped her still body almost to the chin;
And over all a thousand candles flan ed
Against the winking jewels, or streamed down
The marble aisle, and flashed along the guard

Of men-at-arms that slowly wove their turns,
Backward and forward, through the distant gloom.
When Carlo entered, his unsteady feet
Scarce bore him to the altar, and his head
Drooped down so low that all his shining curls
Poured on his breast, and veiled his countenance.
Upon his easel a half-finished work,
The secret labor of his studio,
Said from the canvas, so that none might err,
"I am the Countess Laura." Carlo kneeled,
And gazed upon the picture; as if thus,
Through those clear eyes, he saw the way to
    heaven.
Then he arose; and as a swimmer comes
Forth from the waves, he shook his locks aside,
Emerging from his dream, and standing firm
Upon a purpose with his sovereign will.
He took his palette, murmuring, "Not yet!"
Confidingly and softly to the corpse;
And as the veriest drudge, who plies his art
Against his fancy, he addressed himself
With stolid resolution to his task.
Turning his vision on his memory,
And shutting out the present, till the dead,
The gilded pall, the lights, the pacing guard,
And all the meaning of that solemn scene
Became as nothing, and creative Art
Resolved the whole to chaos, and reformed
The elements according to her law:
So Carlo wrought, as though his eye and hand
Were Heaven's unconscious instruments, and
    worked
The settled purpose of Omnipotence.

And it was wondrous how the red, the white,
The ochre, and the umber, and the blue,
From mottled blotches, hazy and opaque,
Grew into rounded forms and sensuous lines;
How just beneath the lucid skin the blood
Glimmered with warmth; the scarlet lips apart
Bloomed with the moisture of the dews of life;
How the light glittered through and underneath
The golden tresses, and the deep, soft eyes
Became intelligent with conscious thought,
And somewhat troubled underneath the arch
Of eyebrows but a little too intense
For perfect beauty; how the pose and poise
Of the lithe figure on its tiny foot
Suggested life just ceased from motion; so
That any one might cry, in marveling joy,
"That creature lives,—has senses, mind, a soul
To win God's love or dare hell's subtleties!"
The artist paused. The ratifying "Good!"
Trembled upon his lips. He saw no touch
To give or soften. "It is done," he cried,—
"My task, my duty! Nothing now on earth
Can taunt me with a work left unfulfilled!"
The lofty flame, which bore him up so long,
Died in the ashes of humanity;
And the mere man rocked to and fro again
Upon the centre of his wavering heart.
He put aside his palette, as if thus
He stepped from sacred vestments, and assumed
A mortal function in the common world.
"Now for my rights!" he muttered, and approached
The noble body. "O lily of the world!
So withered, yet so lovely! what wast thou

To those who came thus near thee—for I stood
Without the pale of thy half-royal rank—
When thou wast budding, and the streams of life
Made eager struggles to maintain thy bloom,
And gladdened heaven dropped down in gracious
    dews
On its transplanted darling? Hear me now!
I say this but in justice, not in pride,
Not to insult thy high nobility,
But that the poise of things in God's own sight
May be adjusted; and hereafter I
May urge a claim that all the powers of heaven
Shall sanction, and with clarions blow abroad.—
Laura, you loved me! Look not so severe,
With your cold brows, and deadly, close-drawn lips!
You proved it, Countess, when you died for it,—
Let it consume you in the wearing strife
It fought with duty in your ravaged heart.
I knew it ever since that summer-day
I painted Lila, the pale beggar's child,
At rest beside the fountain; when I felt—
Oh, heaven!—the warmth and moisture of your
    breath
Blow through my hair, as with your eager soul—
Forgetting soul and body go as one—
You leaned across my easel till our cheeks—
Ah, me! 'twas not your purpose—touched, and
    clung!
Well, grant 'twas genius; and is genius naught?
I ween it wears as proud a diadem—
Here, in this very world—as that you wear.
A king has held my palette, a grand-duke
Has picked my brush up, and a pope has begged

The favor of my presence in his Rome.
I did not go; I put my fortune by.
I need not ask you why: you knew too well.
It was but natural, it was no way strange,
That I should love you. Everything that saw,
Or had its other senses, loved you, sweet,
And I among them. Martyr, holy saint,—
I see the halo curving round your head,—
I loved you once; but now I worship you,
For the great deed that held my love aloof,
And killed you in the action! I absolve
Your soul from any taint. For from the day
Of that encounter by the fountain-side
Until this moment, never turned on me
Those tender eyes, unless they did a wrong
To nature by the cold, defiant glare
With which they chilled me. Never heard I word
Of softness spoken by those gentle lips;
Never received a bounty from that hand
Which gave to all the world. I know the cause.
You did your duty,—not for honor's sake,
Nor to save sin or suffering or remorse,
Or all the ghosts that haunt a woman's shame,
But for the sake of that pure, loyal love
Your husband bore you. Queen, by grace of God,
I bow before the lustre of your throne!
I kiss the edges of your garment-hem,
And hold myself ennobled! Answer me,—
If I had wronged you, you would answer me
Out of the dusty porches of the tomb:—
Is this a dream, a falsehood? or have I
Spoken the very truth?"—" The very truth!"
A voice replied; and at his side he saw

A form, half shadow and half substance, stand,
Or, rather, rest; for on the solid earth
It had no footing, more than some dense mist
That wavers o'er the surface of the ground
It scarcely touches. With a reverent look,
The shadow's waste and wretched face was bent
Above the picture; as though greater awe
Subdued its awful being, and appalled,
With memories of terrible delight
And fearful wonder, its devouring gaze.
"You make what God makes,—beauty," said the
  shape.
"And might not this, this second Eve, console
 The emptiest heart? Will not this thing outlast
 The fairest creature fashioned in the flesh?
 Before that figure, Time, and Death himself,
 Stand baffled and disarmed. What would you ask
 More than God's power, from nothing to create?"
 The artist gazed upon the boding form,
 And answered: "Goblin, if you had a heart,
 That were an idle question. What to me
 Is my creative power, bereft of love?
 Or what to God would be that selfsame power,
 If so bereaved?"—"And yet the love, thus
  mourned,
 You calmly forfeited. For had you said
 To living Laura—in her burning ears—
 One half that you professed to Laura dead,
 She would have been your own. These contraries
 Sort not with my intelligence. But speak,
 Were Laura living, would the same stale play
 Of raging passion, tearing out its heart
 Upon the rock of duty, be performed?"

" The same, O phantom, while the heart I bear
Trembled, but turned not its magnetic faith
From God's fixed centre."   " If I wake for you
This Laura,—give her all the bloom and glow
Of that midsummer day you hold so dear,—
The smile, the motion, the impulsive soul,
The love of genius,—yea, the very love,
The mortal, hungry, passionate, hot love,
She bore you, flesh to flesh,—would you receive
That gift, in all its glory, at my hands?"
A smile of malice curled the tempter's lips,
And glittered in the caverns of his eyes,
Mocking the answer. Carlo paled and shook ;
A woeful spasm went shuddering through his
    frame,
Curdling his blood, and twisting his fair face
With nameless torture. But he cried aloud,
Out of the clouds of anguish, from the smoke
Of very martyrdom; " O God, she is thine !
Do with her at thy pleasure !" Something grand,
And radiant as a sunbeam, touched the head
He bent in awful sorrow. " Mortal, see"——
" Dare not ! As Christ was sinless, I abjure
These vile abominations ! Shall she bear
Life's burden twice, and life's temptations twice,
While God is justice?" — " Who has made you
    judge
Of what you call God's good, and what you think
God's evil? One to him, the source of both,
The God of good and of permitted ill.
Have you no dream of days that might have been,
Had you and Laura filled another fate ?—
Some cottage on the sloping Apennines,

Roses and lilies, and the rest all love?
I tell you that this tranquil dream may be
Filled to repletion. Speak, and in the shade
Of my dark pinions I shall bear you hence,
And land you where the mountain goat himself
Struggles for footing." He outspread his wings,
And all the chapel darkened, as though hell
Had swallowed up the tapers; and the air
Grew thick, and, like a current sensible,
Flowed round the person, with a wash and dash,
As of the waters of a nether sea.
Slowly and calmly through the dense obscure,
Dove-like and gentle, rose the artist's voice:
"I dare not bring her spirit to that shame!
Know my full meaning.—I who neither fear
Your mystic person nor your dreadful power.
Nor shall I now invoke God's potent name,
For my deliverance from your toils. I stand
Upon the founded structure of his law,
Established from the first, and thence defy
Your arts, reposing all my trust in that!"
The darkness eddied off; and Carlo saw
The figure gathering, as from outer space,
Brightness on brightness; and his former shape
Fell from him, like the ashes that fall off,
And show a core of mellow fire within.
Adown his wings there poured a lambent flood,
That seemed as molten gold, which plashing fell
Upon the floor, enringing him with flame;
And o'er the tresses of his beaming head
Arose a stream of many-colored light,
Like that which crowns the morning. Carlo stood
Steadfast, for all the splendor, reaching up

The outstretched palms of his untainted soul
Towards heaven for strength. A moment thus;
    then asked,
With reverential wonder quivering through
His sinking voice, "Who, spirit, and what art
    thou?"
"I am that blessing which men fly from,—Death."
"Then take my hand, if so God orders it;
For Laura waits me." "But, bethink thee, man,
What the world loses in the loss of thee!
What wondrous art will suffer with eclipse!
What unwon glories are in store for thee!
What fame, outreaching time and temporal shocks,
Would shine upon the letters of thy name
Graven in marble, or the brazen height
Of columns wise with memories of thee!"
"Take me! If I outlived the Patriarchs,
I could but paint those features o'er and o'er:
Lo! that is done." A smile of pity lit
The seraph's features, as he looked to heaven,
With deep inquiry in his tender eyes.
The mandate came. He touched with downy wing
The sufferer lightly on his aching heart;
And gently, as the sky-lark settles down
Upon the clustered treasures of her nest,
So Carlo softly slid along the prop
Of his tall easel, nestling at the foot
As though he slumbered; and the morning broke
In silver whiteness over Padua.

THE FIDDLER.

"FIDDLER, fiddle me something gay,
  Something bright as a summer day,
Something to draw the sting of pain
Out of a mortal's heart and brain!"
So spake the Knight, a beggar he,
Ousted, and hurled from his high degree,
When the foeman clambered his castle-wall,
And hustled him over, squires and all.
Those were the days of ups and downs,
Of bloody fingers and cloven crowns.
Never a thought had they of law,
Of a title's strength or a parchment's flaw;
Everything was settled straight
By a lance's thrust or a bilbo's weight;
And in such a settlement, I wis,
Our Knight lost all that he once called his.
Nothing now remained to him
Save the tattered Fiddler, crooked and grim,
Who stuck to his skirts, in fate's despite,
And followed him round as the day the night.
So the little Fiddler bent his ear,
And tuned and tuned, till the strings rang clear;
And then he rosined his horse-hair braid,
And this was the way the Fiddler played.
He played till the birds came screaming round,
  And the flowers leaped up from the gaping ground,—

Shot, leaved and budded, and in a wink
Were paling or blushing in white or pink.
He played till you saw the trailers crawl,
Like lizards over a shady wall,
And hang their blossoms in wreaths and bands,
As though 'twere the work of festal hands.
He played until the staid old trees
Loosened their boughs to the laughing breeze,
And danced in circles of giddy mirth,
Tearing their roots from the startled earth.
He played until the secret things,
That hide in fissures, on gauzy wings
Buzzed round and round through the drunken air,
And the toads leaped forth from their clammy lair.
Nothing so timid, nothing so bold,
But eddied and whirled as the music rolled.
The hare tripped out from her dark retreat;
The panther purred at his very feet;
The owl for a moment tried to look
Grave, till his ruffled feathers shook
With crazy laughter; the cool-veined snakes
Flickered their tongues through the thorny brakes,
And whirled and twisted and squirmed their tails,
And glittered the gems of their lucid scales.
Ah me! such madness, such helpless mirth.
Was a sight to see on the stolid earth!—
A sight so strange that the citizens
Came creeping out from their gloomy dens;
And the rustics dropped their laboring tools,
Grinning and winking—the simple fools!—
Till the music changed, by so slow a pace
That none might say where the change took place;

THE FIDDLER.

For something between a sigh and groan
Labored and surged through the undertone,—
A sob of sorrow, a wail of pain,
That rose and faded, and rose again;
Ever becoming more and more
Plain, like the tide's advancing roar,
Till with a sudden burst and shock,
That shook the frame of the founded rock,
Hissing and howling, the wave shot high,
And scattered its brine in the quailing eye.
Misery, misery! how they wept,
As the flood of music o'er them swept!
As when the jaws of the hungry sea
Closed on the Theban chivalry,
And armored soldier and harnessed horse
Tossed up to heaven a floundering corse,
And Miriam's cymbals flashed and pealed
Over Jehovah's battle-field.
Caught in the toils were the silly sheep:
They came to laugh, but they stayed to weep.
They thought because the world was gay
At the crooked Fiddler's mystic lay,
That they could giggle and mend their cheer,
And hear his tones with the selfsame ear.
What of the Knight who caused this woe,
By his careless mandate long ago?—
What of the Knight? He paid his score;
He had been dead an hour or more.
But the music bated not a jot,
Floating away o'er town and cot;
Climbing to heaven in golden mist,
Till the serving cherubs cried, "Oh hist!"

Bending their earnest faces low,
And nodding in time to the music's flow:
And for aught the tongue of man can say,
The little Fiddler will fiddle away
Till the sun turns black on the judgment-day.

AD CRITICUM.

WHY harp upon a well-worn string
    Whose note is flat and out of tune?
Why take the morning skylark's wing,
    And sing his song at blazing noon?

The world grows sage. The harmless tales
    That took her in her infant years,
Now stretch her patience till it fails,
    And weary her averted ears.

What thing, in sooth, hast thou to tell,
    Thou dreamer in a world awake?—
Dost thou not hear the factory-bell,
    And feel the panting engine shake?

What swiftest thought of art's desire
    But droops with shame, and feebly lags
Behind the intellectual wire
    That tells the price of corn and rags?

I answer not; I marvel much;
    I see no issue, save for ill,
In that which gives creative touch,
    Yet lets the moral man stand still.

AD CRITICUM.

Strong Science strides he knows not where—
   He knows not where, he knows not why;
Blind Samson, with his new-grown hair,
   Tugs at the pillars of the sky.

Those pillars that our heaven sustained—
   Imagination, faith, love, law—
Are crumbling at the base, and veined
   Throughout with many a ghastly flaw.

What beauty crowns the smoking gorge,
   Or from the laboring river steals,
Where grins the glaring smutty forge,
   Or spin a thousand buzzing wheels?

To me this landscape, bought and sold,
   This peddled earth, put up to sell,
This weary, endless clink of gold
   Is drearier than the passing bell.

I sicken at the moral dearth
   That prates of progress, in a day
When all the holiest things of earth
   Are stealthy Mammon's lawful prey.

'Tis well for you beyond the sea,
   Where every toiling mattock delves
Among the spoils of history,
   To bid us work within ourselves.

All bare of legendary lore
   Our grandest regions stretch away;
These are the pictured scenes, no more—
   These are the scenery, not the play.

AD CRITICUM.

The glories which a view puts on,
   Within the gazer's feeling lie;
A great deed on a hillock done,
   May lift it till it touch the sky.

Who ever calls the Avon strait,
   Or dwarfs the head of old Skiddaw,
Who looks in Shakespeare's book of fate,
   Or bends to Wordsworth's kindly law?

Who questions now the sovereign right
   That drew from Greek and Roman lore,
Or dares to jeer at the weird light
   That shines round castled Elsinore?

The Jew of Venice walks the Strand,
   The Moor displays his tawny birth;
For England seems no alien land
   To these great citizens of earth.

Not here nor there, in Ariel's pine,
   On teeming Nile, in Timon's cell,
Where Juliet's nightly beauties shine,
   Or fate grows dark round Isabel,—

No, nor to any time, howe'er
   Remote or strange, can be confined
These human hearts whose boundless sphere
   But broadens with the general mind.

He with art's mystery poorly deals,
   Who cramps within a narrow band
That whose ethereal nature feels
   The strength of God's sustaining hand.

Not for myself, but for my art
   I claim all ages, every clime ;
And I shall scorn the lines that part
   Country from country, time from time.

O Poet of the present day !
   Range back or forth, change time or place,
But mould the sinews of your lay
   To struggle in the final race !

Your triumph in the end stands clear ;
   For when a few short years have run,
The past, the present, there and here,
   To future times will be as one.

DIRGE FOR A SAILOR.

SLOW, slow! toll it low,
    As the sea-waves break and flow;
With the same dull, slumberous motion
As his ancient mother, Ocean,
    Rocked him on, through storm and calm,
    From the iceberg to the palm:
    So his drowsy ears may deem
    That the sound which breaks his dream
    Is the ever-moaning tide
    Washing on his vessel's side.

    Slow, slow! as we go
    Swing his coffin to and fro;
As of old the lusty billow
Swayed him on his heaving pillow:
    So that he may fancy still,
    Climbing up the watery hill,
    Plunging in the watery vale,
    With her wide-distended sail,
    His good bark securely stands
    Onward to the golden lands.

    Slow, slow! heave-a-ho!
    Lower him to the mould below
With the well-known sailor chorus,
Lest he paler grow before us

At the thought that Ocean's child,
From his mother's arms beguiled,
Must repose for countless years,
Reft of all her briny tears,
All the rights he owned by birth,
In the dusty lap of earth.

ISABEL.

A DIRGE.

Isabel, Isabel,
This is dreary work—ah, well!—
Dreary work to weave in verse
Something to bedeck thy hearse:
I who fain would only weep,
Gazing on thee, laid to sleep
By a spell the ages keep.

Isabel, Isabel,
When thy footsteps lightly fell
On the May-day flowers, less fair
Than thy virgin graces were,
Little did I think the vow,
Made to thee with laughing brow,
Would be kept at last as now.

Isabel, Isabel,
Thus you said: " O ring my knell!
Never sing of any one
Till these mortal sands be run:
Beauty flees and leaves no trace;
Honor changes to disgrace;
Death alone can crown the race."

Isabel, Isabel,
I have kept thy counsel well.
Though my heart sang night and day,
Not a word my lips would say;
Though I saw thy beauties grow,
And thy virtues, pure as snow,
Whiten all thy life below.

Isabel, Isabel,
Since that fatal day befell,
I, who now have leave to speak,
Stand in sorrow dumb and weak.
Go!—'tis better—lips above
Sing to thee, thou spotless dove,
All thou once denied to love!

A DIRGE.

Let me clothe my limbs with sackcloth, and strew ashes o'er my head;
Let me close the doors of mourning, lest this wretched thing be said:
Lo! the hearth is cold and naked, and its light for ever fled!

Let me dig thy grave, unwitnessed, in the lingering winter snow,
And conceal thee as a treasure; so that none alive may know
What the world has lost, or whither its supremest creatures go.

I could never think thee mortal: when I looked into thine eyes,
I beheld a wondrous vision through the gates of Paradise—
All the light, the life ecstatic, of the fulgent inner skies.

Nay, thou art not dead as others: thou hast only lent thy worth
To make beautiful and vital what was once but senseless earth,
And thou'lt give its dust a spirit, an immortal second birth.

For since earth contains thy beauty, she has grown
 a holier thing;
She will waken fairer, sweeter, in the coming days
 of spring,
When the early blossoms open, and the wandering
 songs take wing.

We shall see within the violet thy glittering lids
 unclose;
In the lily-of-the-valley shall thy purity repose;
And yet later thou shalt triumph in the splendor of
 the rose:

So that men will say thy footsteps must have been
 among the flowers,
And will fail to miss thee wholly, through thy gift
 to nature's powers,
In the long, soft summer mornings and the tranquil
 evening hours.

Only I shall have the secret, and the fatal truth shall
 know,
By this grave I dig to hide thee in the tardy winter
 snow—
By this vacant desolation—by this utter, endless
 woe!

SONG.

BREATHE, violets, breathe! blow, primrose
 beds,
 Along the gliding streams!
Breathe low, blow meekly, modest heads;
 Flow, brooks, in silent dreams!

She comes, the sweetest, fairest flower,
 The lightest moving grace,
To perfume heaven, to bloom an hour
 Within our trysting-place.

O violet sweet, and primrose bright,
 And softly falling tide,
Where are your charms, that won my sight,
 Now she is by my side?

PATRIOTIC POEMS.

OUR HEROIC THEMES.

READ BEFORE THE PHI BETA KAPPA SOCIETY OF HARVARD UNIVERSITY,

July 20, 1865.

TURN as I may in search of worthy themes,
To fill with life the poet's solemn dreams, —
Some hint from Rome, some retrospect of Greece,
Red with their war, or golden with their peace;
Some thought of Lancelot and Guinevere,
The "arm in samite" and the "mystic mere";
Or those grand echoes that for ever flow
From Roland's horn through narrow Roncesvaux;
Some spark yet living of the strange romance
Whose flame illumined the Crusader's lance;
Or that strong purpose which unclosed the seas
Before the vision of the Genoese;
Or when the love-lock and the close-cropped crown
Died with a laugh, or triumphed with a frown;
Or the frail Mayflower poured her prayerful flock
Upon the breast of Plymouth's wintry rock;
Or when the children of these hardy men
Bearded the throne they never loved again; —
Something I sought, whose wonted sound might call
Familiar echoes from this learnéd hall;
But sought in vain. The Past, unreal and far,
Loomed through the dusty vapors of our war,

And what was clear before my boyish glance
Lost, for the man, its old significance.
Those splendid themes, so sacred to my youth,—
Those dreams of fancy with their heart of truth,—
Paled as I viewed them in the fresher rays
That light the scenes of these heroic days;
Shrank, as the young Colossus of our age
With scornful finger turned the historic page,
And sought, through pigmy chiefs and pigmy wars,
To peer his stature and his dreadful scars,—
Sought till a smile o'erran his studious frown,
Then razed the records as he wrote his own:
Matchless in grandeur, product of a cause
As deep and changeless as those moral laws
That base themselves upon the throne of God,—
Fair with His blessings, awful with His rod.
Find me in history, since Adam fell,
This story's rival or its parallel:
A nation rising to undo a wrong
Forged by itself, and to its mind made strong
By every word its angry tongue had hurled
In stout defiance at a sneering world.
Since Paul was stricken on Damascus' plain,
Brimming with mischief and contrivings vain,
And God's dread brightness sealed his mortal sight,
But fired his spirit with a heavenly light,
Such swift conversion has not entered in
The darkened vision of unconscious sin,
As when this nation, in its proudest glow,
Reeled, weak and blinded, with the sudden blow;
But saw — thank God! — truth's inward ray make plain
The old delusions of its erring brain;

And even as Paul, from Ananias' hands,
Received his vision and his Lord's commands,
So, changed and contrite, sank the nation down
Before thy touch of glory, brave John Brown!

But why explore the sources of the flood,
Whence all the land ran steel and fire and blood?
My heart is fretting, like a tethered steed,
To join the hero in his noble deed.
A noise of armies gathers in my ears,
The Southern yells, the Northern battle-cheers;
The endless volleys, ceaseless as the roar
Of the vexed ocean brawling with its shore;
The groaning cannon, puffing at a breath
Man's shreds and fragments through the jaws of death;
The rush of horses, and the whirring sway
Of the keen sabre cleaving soul from clay;
And over all, intelligible and clear
As spoken language to a listening ear,
The trumpet orders the tumultuous herds,
And leads the flocks of battle with its words.
'Twas mine to witness and to feel the shame
Manasses cast upon our early fame,
When the raw greenness of our boastful bands
Yielded a victory almost in their hands;
Fled from the field before a vanquished foe,
And lied about it, to complete the woe.
Since then, through all the changes of the war,
My eyes have followed our ascending star.—
Ascending ever, though at times the cloud
Of dark disaster casts its murky shroud
About our guide, oppressing men with fear
Lest the last day of liberty drew near;—

Through all I knew, and with my faith upborne
Turned on the weak a smile of pitying scorn,
That our calm star still filled its destined place,
Lost to our sight, but shining in God's face.

With growing courage, day by day I hung
Above the soldier of the quiet tongue.
Sneers hissed about him, penmen fought his war;
Here he was lacking, there he went too far.
Alas! how bloody! But, alack! how tame!
O for Lee's talent!—O ye fools, for shame!
From the first move, his foe defensive stood;
And was that nothing? It was worth the blood.
O chief supreme, the head of glory's roll!
O will of steel, O lofty, generous soul,
Sharing thy laurels, lest a comrade want;
Why should I name thee? Every mouth cries,
    Grant!

Firm was my faith in him whose sturdy skill
Three dreadful days had held the quaking hill;
Stood like a rock on which the fiery spray
Beat out its life, then slowly ebbed away;
Saved our domain from rapine, waste and wrath,
And taught the foe an unreturning path,—
Light of our darkness, succor of our need,
God of our country, bless the name of Meade!

I watched with Thomas while his wary glance
Marked the rash foes their heedless lines advance;
Step after step he lured their willing feet
Into the toils, from whence was no retreat;

Then with a swoop, as when the eagle swings
Out of his eyrie, with the roar of wings,
The veteran fell upon his venturous prey,—
And—let Hood end it, if there's aught to say.

I saw with wonder Sherman's Titan line
Pour from the mountains to the distant brine,
Sweep treason's cradle bare of all its brood,
And turn its garden to a solitude.
Fear ran before him, Famine groaned behind,
And, following Famine, came the humble mind.

Who felt a care within his bosom grow,
Of more than pity for the hapless foe,
Or spent a fear on that which Fate's decrees
Already wrote amongst her victories,
When in the tumult of the battled van
Shone Fortune's darling, mounted Sheridan?
Rapid to plan and peerless in the fight,
He plucked Fame's chaplet as by sovereign right;
Emerged triumphant from a wild retreat,
And blazoned victory's colors on defeat.

I marked the navy lay its iron hand
Upon the waves, and clutch the trembling land;
Heard the stern music of Dupont resound,
To time the measures of his fiery round;
Or Foot's fierce clamor, as his flaming breath
Sounded a challenge in the face of death.
Saw Morris rising from the wreck-strewn sea,
Crowned with more fame than beams from victory;
Or foe-girt Winslow, ocean's errant knight,
Dare Treason's champion to a single fight;

Or Porter thunder with his shot and shell
Upon the foe's last crumbling citadel:
Or—let us pause before that height we scale,
Where stands a title that makes others pale;
That so much tried the stretching arm of Fame,
She stood on tiptoe when she wrote his name.
Captor of cities and of sovereign States,
Whose prow unlocked the rivers' armèd gates;
Whose starry ensign ruled the troubled sky,
And waved o'er earth the rod of destiny.
Ever victorious, he but raised his hand,
And cringing Fortune lackeyed his command.
What name but one shall I pronounce to clear
My tongue from flattery in the public ear?
The land replies from palace, farm and hut;—
Need I proclaim it?—David Farragut!

Through anxious years I saw the martial flood
Surge back and forth in waves of fire and blood.
Sometimes it paused, and sometimes seemed to reel,
Spent and exhausted, from the rebel steel;
But every shock was sapping, blow by blow,
The bars that backward held the overflow;
Till suddenly the ruin cracked and roared,
And over all the human torrent poured!
Then bloomed the harvest of our patient aims;
Then bowed the world before our deeds and names;
Then on the proudest of Fame's temple-gates
Shone novel records and thick-crowded dates.
New wreaths were hung upon her hornèd shrines,
New clarions blown before her martial lines;
Fresh incense smoked and fresh libations dripped;
The vernal laurels from the hills were stripped,

And woven in chaplets. Far and near the hum
Of gladness ushered the returning drum.
Welcome stood beckoning, looking towards the South,
With cheers of transport brimming in the mouth;
Till came the rapture of that crowning hour,
When the vast armies poured their awful power
In dense procession through the marble banks,
That rang and quivered with a nation's thanks;
While, like a temple of the morning sky,—
August, sublime, refulgent, calm and high,—
Towered in its might, as symbol of the whole,
The dome-crowned presence of the Capitol.
I envy those whose tattered standards waved
Within the city which their valor saved,—
The Eastern heroes and their Western peers,—
The holy joy that glittered in their tears,
As thronging upward to the nation's throne,
They knelt, and sobbed, and kissed the very stone.
And thou, brave army, that hast borne the brunt
Of stern defeat so often on thy front,—
Thou who hast rallied from each stunning blow,
With godlike patience facing still the foe,—
Thou moving pivot of the deadly fight,
Whose steadfast centre held all things aright,—
Twice saved us from the foe's audacious feet,
And drove him howling through his last retreat,—
Hung on his steps until for peace he knelt,
And sued for mercy which he never felt!—
I thank fair Fortune that it was thy fate
Alone to hurl the traitors from their state;
Alone to make their capital thy prize,
And watch the treason close its bloody eyes!

O roll, Potomac, prouder of thy name,
Touched by the splendor of thy army's fame!
Thrill with the steps of thy returning braves,
Wail through thy margins of uncounted graves,
Laugh at the echo of thy soldiers' shout,
Whisper their story to the lands about,
Yea, feel each passion of the human soul,
But roll, great river, in thy glory roll!

We who have watched the fortunes of this war,
Whate'er our faith, securely and afar,
Should blush like girls to see our soldiers come
Behind their colors and their boy-borne drum;
And think that we bore neither gun nor sword,
But gave our country—what?—an idle word,
As through the terrors of the fiery strife
She plunged, sore panting for her very life.
This was no war to soothe a monarch's pride;
Angels and devils struggled on each side;
Tugged hand in hand, with hot, ferocious breath;
The prize existence, and the forfeit death;
While human freedom, for the whole world's sake,
Hung, like a martyr, at the gory stake.

The moral issue stood sublime and clear
Above the strife, above mere hope or fear;
What men might compass, to our hands was given:
But as we strove, we wrought the work of Heaven.
Crown we our heroes with a holier wreath
Than man e'er wore upon this side of death;
Mix with their laurels deathless asphodels,
And chime their pæans from the sacred bells!

Nor in your prayers forget the martyred Chief,
Fallen for the gospel of your own belief,
Who, ere he mounted to the people's throne,
Asked for your prayers, and joined in them his own.
I knew the man. I see him, as he stands
With gifts of mercy in his outstretched hands;
A kindly light within his gentle eyes,
Sad as the toil in which his heart grew wise;
His lips half parted with the constant smile
That kindled truth, but foiled the deepest guile;
His head bent forward, and his willing ear
Divinely patient right and wrong to hear:
Great in his goodness, humble in his state,
Firm in his purpose, yet not passionate,
He led his people with a tender hand,
And won by love a sway beyond command.
Summoned by lot to mitigate a time
Frenzied with rage, unscrupulous with crime,
He bore his mission with so meek a heart
That Heaven itself took up his people's part;
And when he faltered, helped him ere he fell,
Eking his efforts out by miracle.
No king this man, by grace of God's intent;
No, something better, freeman,—President!
A nature modeled on a higher plan,
Lord of himself, an inborn gentleman!

Pass by his fate. Forget the closing strife
In the vast memories of his noble life.
Forget the scene, the bravo stealing nigh,
The pistol-shot, the new-made widow's cry,
The palsied people, and the tears that ran
O'er half a world to mourn a single man.

But O remember, while the mind can hold
One record sacred to the days of old,
The gentle heart that beat its life away
Just as young morning donned his robe of gray,
Stole through the tears beneath his golden tread,
And touched in vain the eyelids of the dead!
Remember him, as one who died for right
With victory's trophies glittering in his sight;
His mission finished, and the settled end
Assured and owned by stranger, foe and friend.
Nothing was left him but to taste the sweet
Of triumph sitting in the nation's seat;
And for that triumph Heaven prepared its courts,
And cleared its champaigns for unwonted sports;
Summoned the spirits of the noble dead
Who fell in battle for the cause he led:
Soldiers and chiefs awakened from the clay,
And ranged their legions in the old array.
There Lyon led, and Kearny rode amain,
And wise McPherson drew his bridle-rein;
Brave Reynolds marshaled his undaunted corps,
And Sedgwick pressed to reach the front once more.
The star of Mitchell glittered over all,
And Stevens answered Reno's bugle-call.
Bayard looked worthy of his knightly name,
And Mansfield's eyes were bright with battle-flame.
Lander's grand brow was flushed with eager ire,
And Strong arose from Wagner's roaring fire.
There gallant Buford in the van was seen,
And Corcoran waved his flag of Irish green.
Birney's clear eyes were radiant with his faith;
Winthrop and Greble dared a second death.

Down Shaw's dark front a solemn purpose ran,—
The slave's resolve to prove himself—mere man;
The hero's courage for that humble hope
Was all that winged him up the bloody slope.
There burly Nelson blustered through his men,
And Richardson deployed his lines again.
Baker looked thoughtful; Wadsworth's liberal hand
Pointed right forward; and the sharp command
Of Smith's wild valor bore his soldiers on,
As when it rang o'er fated Donelson!

All these, and more, before the Martyr's gaze
Passed through the shout of heaven's tumultuous
    praise,
The sound of clarions, and the choral songs
Of rapture bursting from the seraph throngs,—
Passed, like a pageant from the evening skies,
But left a picture on celestial eyes,
Whose tints shall mellow as the days increase,
And shine a marvel in the Realm of Peace;—
Outlast the stir and bustle of our race,
When earth has vanished from her ancient place,
And naught survives in all eternity
Save faded fragments of our history,
And this angelic legend, told of one
Sprung from a planet cycles since undone:
"Yon human spirit, with the tender eyes,
  God welcomed here with high solemnities;
Gave him a triumph, until then unknown,
He standing meekly close beside the Throne."

CAPTAIN SEMMES, C. S. A. N.

June 19, 1864.

OUT of Cherbourg harbor one clear
    Sunday morning the cavalier,
Captain Semmes, with his cap a-cock,
Sailed from the friendly Frenchman's dock.
Gayly along the rebel came,
Under the flag of the cross of shame;
Knight of the handcuff and bloody lash,
He twirled the point of his red moustache,
And swore in English, not over nice,
To sink our Yankee scum in a trice,
Or burn our ship, as the thing might be,
Where the eyes of Cherbourg all should see.
    "Heigh-ho! you don't say so!"
Whispered his friend, little Jean Crapaud.

Semmes had been a wolf of the deep
For many a day to harmless sheep;
Ships he scuttled and robbed and burned,
Watches pilfered and pockets turned;
And all his plunder, bonds and gold,
He left for his Gallic friend to hold.
A little over-prudent was he
For a cavalier of high degree;
And Raphael Semmes don't sound, indeed,
As though it came of the purple seed;

But all the blood in his veins was blue,
And his clay was porcelain through and through.
    Heigh-ho! the Lord doth know
We are but dirt, and our blood's so-so.

What will the doughty Captain do
With his British ship, his British crew,
His gunners, trained in the " Excellent,"
The guns his cousin Blakely sent,
His shot and shell at Woolwich made,—
What will he do with the whole parade?
Up to the top of his cliffs Crapaud
Had clambered to see the Sunday show;
And his brother Bull, in his fancy yacht,
Stood off and on towards the fated spot;
And right across the bold Captain's way
The Kearsarge steamed in her war array.
    " Heigh-ho!" said Semmes—" Let's blow
That craft to splinters before we go."

Semmes had heard, with his lip a-curl,
In Cherbourg, that some Northern churl,
Backed by a gang of onion-eaters,
Waited the noble negro-beaters.
Shop-keeping, peddling, vulgar knaves,
To stick their heads into open graves!
" 'Sdeath! 'swounds! 'ods bodkins! Ha! what then,
Will they dare to fight with gentlemen?
O, had I my lance and shield and things,
With which I tilted at Sulphur Springs!
Or a troop of horse marines! Of course,
A knight is nothing without his horse."
    Heigh-ho! this seemed to show
Our hero's spirits were running low.

Straight out to sea the Kearsarge drew,
And Semmes, who followed all that flew,
Followed, perhaps by some mistake,
Close in his foeman's frothing wake.
But when three leagues were gained from shore,
Slowly and grimly the Yankee wore,
And our starry ensign leaped above,
Round which the wind, like a fluttering dove,
Cooed low, and the sunshine of God's day
Like an open blessing on it lay;
So we felt our friendless ship would fight
Full under the great Disposer's sight.
  Heigh-ho! 'tis well to know
Who looks on the deeds done here below.

Semmes led the waltz and struck the tune;
Shots at the sea and at the moon
The swashing, wasteful cavalier
Scattered around him far and near.
The saving Yankees squandered not
An ounce of powder or pound of shot:
They held their peace till the guns would tell,
Then out they burst like the mouths of hell.
Terrible, horrible! how they tore
The Alabama, until the gore
From her bursting scuppers smoked and streamed,
The dying groaned and the wounded screamed!
  "Heigh-ho!" said Semmes, "let's show
These Yankees the heels we boast of so."

Seven times in that deadly round
Sped the ships to the cannon's sound.
The vulture, through the smoke and din,
Saw the eagle's circles narrowing in;

And every time her pivots roared
The fatal bomb-shells came straight aboard.
His helm was useless, his engine failed,
His powder was wet, his Britons quailed;
And in his course, like a warning hand,
Stretched forth the flag of his outraged land.
In vain he hoisted his sails to flee;
For each foot he sailed, his foe sailed three.
  Heigh-ho! "Why, here's a blow!"
Said Semmes, as he hauled his flag below.

Well was it for the cavalier
That Brother Bull was lying near;
His vessel with a haughty curl
Turned up her nose, and in the whirl
Of the white sea stern foremost tore,
As if in scorn of the crew she bore.
Then the thrifty Briton launched his boat,
To pick up aught that might be afloat,
And amongst other less precious spoil,
Fished swordless Semmes from his watery coil.
"Hide me!" the gallant cried in affright;
"Cover me up from the Yankee's sight!"
  Heigh-ho! they laid him low,
With a bit of sail to hide his woe.

Safely they bore the chief aboard,
Leaving behind his fame and sword;
And then the Deerhound stole away,
Lest Winslow's guns might have a say;
Landed him in Southampton town,
Where heroes like him have had renown,
Ever since Lawrence, Perry and Hull
Took hold of the horns of great John Bull.

Had I been Winslow, I say to you,
As the sea is green, the sky is blue,
Through the Deerhound I'd have sent a shot,
And John might have liked the thing or not.
     Heigh-ho! come soon or slow,
In the end we are bound to have a blow.

What said the Frenchman from his hill
After the cannon-shots were still?
What said the Briton from his deck,
Gazing down on the sunken wreck?
Something was said of guns like mortars,
And something of smooth-bores at close quarters;
Chain armor furnished a word or two;
But the end of all was both looked blue.
They sighed again o'er the "Great Contention."
But never hinted at "Intervention."
One thing they wished, which they dared not say,
"If the fight had but gone the other way!
     Heigh-ho! I told you so!
Oh, Semmes was a sorry fool to go!"

CAVALRY SHERIDAN.

September 19, 1864.

I.

SHERIDAN, Sheridan, Cavalry Sheridan!
  Him of the horses and sabres I sing.
    Look, how he drove them!
    Look, how he clove them!
Sabred, belabored, confused and confounded
The whole rebel rout, as they fell back astounded
    At the fierce stride and swing
    Of our men galloping,
Shouting with vengeance, roaring with laughter,
Cheering with victory as they plunged after
Sheridan, Sheridan, Cavalry Sheridan!

II.

Ah, fair Shenandoah, thou nest of the robber,
  How stands the count with thy people to-day?
    Where is the fire now,
    Showing thy ire now,
Blazing, while gazing with fear and amazement,
As on it crept swiftly from door-post to casement,
    Weeping with pale dismay,
    Stood maids and matrons gray?
Has it not spread to thy end of the valley?
Did it not follow thee in thy grand sally,
Sheridan, Sheridan, Cavalry Sheridan?

III.

Chambersburg, Chambersburg, smouldering Chambersburg,
  Sit in thy ruins, content with thy lot!
    Lo, thy despoiler,
    Snared by the toiler,
Retreated defeated—torn, pierced, slashed with gashes—
And what thy homes were, now their bodies are —ashes!
    O, be thy griefs forgot;
    Every bright laureled spot
On thy fair hill-sides wait matron and maiden
With chaplets of glory, to welcome and laden
Sheridan, Sheridan, Cavalry Sheridan!

IV.

O Early, mad Early, thou ruthless invader,
  Where are the troopers who followed thy raid?
    Look at their corses!
    Soldiers and horses
Whiten and brighten with bones, shining grimly,
On all the wide plains they rode over so trimly.
    What has the raven said?
    Where has the red fox preyed?
What is the high-sailing buzzard declaring
In Richmond's white upturned face of thy warfaring,
Sheridan, Sheridan, Cavalry Sheridan?

V.

Sheridan, Sheridan, Cavalry Sheridan,
  When thou shalt come to thy people again,

Crowns we shall twine for thee;
And the ripe wine for thee,
Flashing and splashing from goblet and beaker,
Shall whirl round the lips of the eloquent speaker,
As he essays in vain
Homage to make it plain
How the great heart of the jubilant nation
Swells towards thy own in its full admiration,
Sheridan, Sheridan, Cavalry Sheridan!

FORT FISHER.

January 15, 1865.

BRIGHT as the sun of Austerlitz,
    Rose the sun that winter day;
A sky as clear as burnished steel
    Round his golden circle lay.

Across the track of glittering green
    Which his level glances swept,
Like a conscious thing in happy dreams,
    The crystal ocean slept.

The surf was still upon the beach,
    Save the pulse of that endless swell
Which rattled the pebbles in its foam,
    And tumbled the painted shell.

A low breeze crept from off the land,
    And fluttered, and then was dumb,
As through our drowsy fleet it shook
    The sound of the rebel drum.

Flash! crash! At once the flag-ship woke,
    Like a monster of the deep
That starts from night-long, wave-rocked rest,
    And spurns away his sleep.

So in an instant all alive
    The ship of the Admiral seemed,
As flocking up from deck to peak,
    His signal colors streamed.

The dark, grim sisters of the waves
    Held council for a while,
Then with bowed heads, in clouds of smoke,
    Swooped landward file on file.

A torrent foamed at every bow,
    In each wake a frothing brook,
And at every pant each fiery heart
    In their oaken bosoms shook.

Before the mounds of Fisher rolled,
    Crouched down on their spit of sand;
Behind them stretched the clutching lines
    Of our Terry's iron hand.

Close in the fleet of armored ships,
    At their work already set,
Hurled their great shells and ponderous bolts
    Through casemate and parapet.

How the roar deepened, as our guns
    Were joined in the fearful sport!
A thousand pieces, aimed as one,
    That blazed at the crumbling fort.

From early dawn until the sun
    O'erpassed his point of noon,
No music danced in rebel ears
    Save the cannons' awful tune.

No prospect met the rebel gaze
   Save the smoke of bursting shell,
And the dust and rush of sliding earth
   As their walls and bomb-proofs fell.

Their guns, dismounted, round them lay,
   And the ports were choked with sand;
No living thing a breathing space
   On the open works could stand.

It seemed as though a storm of fire
   Had burst from the cloudless skies,
And dreadful shapes thronged through the smoke
   With death in their lurid eyes.

At early evening came a lull,
   For the ships were changing face,
And a hundred barges specked the sea,
   And crowded the landing-place.

Then, as the rabbits limp abroad,
   When their burrows spring has warmed,
So from their lairs the rebels crept,
   And above the ramparts swarmed.

Onward with cheers the sailors dashed,
   But long ere that day was done,
Sore sighed they for the friendly deck,
   And the post beside the gun.

Bravely through ball and shell they stormed,
   Through grape-shot and shrapnel shrill,
But the deadly gun-blasts blew their ranks
   Like chaff from the winnowing-mill.

Preston and Porter vainly fell,
  And Lamson and Bache; in vain
The sands were tracked with blood, and heaped
  With the wounded and the slain.

Backward, as men who yield to fate,
  And yet scorn the deed of shame;
Slowly, with oaths of surly rage,
  To their boats our sailors came.

What flutters o'er the northern wall?
  Look now, where the smoke breaks through!
Huzza! huzza! 'tis Terry's flag—
  'Tis the battle-flag of blue!

And by its side another flies,
  All pierced and gashed with scars;
See, how it flashes through the smoke—
  The grand old stripes and stars!

Ah! then we knew that not in vain
  Had our slaughtered shipmates bled;
And we smiled, as if they also knew,
  In the faces of the dead.

Hark, hark! there goes the steady roll
  Of the calm, well-ordered fire,
From veterans of a hundred fights,
  That will never ebb nor tire.

Curtis had won the foremost mounds
  That sheltered the rebel van,
And down across the traverses
  He followed them man to man.

Each mound was as a battle-field,
    And reeked with its bloody strife;
And not a foot of ground was gained
    That cost not a hero's life.

Shouting and panting, hand to hand,
    They fought till the close of day,
Till the solemn moon among her stars
    Looked down on the dreadful fray.

Curtis closed up his wasted ranks,
    And paused for a final blow;
The bayonets gleamed, and the leveled steel
    Was turned on the stubborn foe.

Then Abbott's shouts rang from the rear,
    As his rushing files came on;
But when we looked for the enemy,
    His broken lines were gone.

A fellow to the cheer we gave
    In the world was never heard;
It made the blood dance in our veins,
    And our matted locks it stirred.

They knew its meaning in the fleet;
    And before our signals glared,
Rockets were leaping up the sky,
    And a thousand blue-lights flared.

A feast of lanterns starred the sea,
    As he kissed the land with bliss;
And the starlight and the moonlight joined
    Their joy in that holy kiss.

Thus was Fort Fisher stormed and won;
And this planet may grow gray
Ere song or chronicle shall tire
With the glories of that day.

ODE ON THANKSGIVING DAY.

December 7, 1865.

SEE how the steeples rock!
    See how the belfries quiver!
Hark to the great bell's shock,
    And the small bell's merry shiver!
And now the quaking air
    Roars with repeated thunder,
As the fiery sobs of the cannon tear
    Their brazen lips asunder!
But a deeper tone ascends
    Than the bell's or the cannon's sounds,
As the bare-browed Nation bends,
    In her tears and her ghastly wounds,
To Him who shapes our ends
Through the battles of sea and plain,
    Who casts His might
    On the side of right,
And has saved our country again!

Therefore ring on, ye jocund bells!
    Join all your airy hands,
    And dance your rounds
    Of intermingled sounds,
Until our hillsides and our grassy dells

Grow green beneath your tread,
And " Peace, Peace, Peace !" be sped
On every breeze that sweeps the dewy lands!
O let the great hearts of the cannon break
    With stress of very gladness,
The rivers tremble and the mountains shake,
    And the drear woods forget their sadness!
And you, ye multitude of sad-eyed men,
Ye homeless orphans and ye widowed wives,
Ye maidens, shadowed in your opening lives
By the dark cloud that will not lift again,—
    Take heart once more!
Throw by your mourning for a single day;
Deck brow and breast with garlands gay;
    Into the sunshine pour,
    And clap your wasted palms,
    And sweeten the sweet psalms
With sacred passion, with that awful faith
Which makes as crystal the dark gates of Death!

    The sacrifice was not in vain,
Nor the sharp anguish, nor the long, long pain.
    No drop of all the bloody rain
    Fell upon barren earth.
    Close to their country's breast
    Each bleeding heart was pressed,
And every pang foretold a giant birth.
    Each grief that found a cry
    Rose through the lucid sky,
A holier incense and a deeper prayer
Than priests can utter from the altar's glare.
    What sacrifice can peer
The soldier's heart-blood and his widow's tear?

ODE ON THANKSGIVING DAY.

What rite so sacred, since the world began,
    As that in which life-loving youth
Takes Death's cold chalice from the hand of Truth;
    Or in the fearful battle's van,
Shouts Freedom's war-cry with his dying will,
Flinging her starry banner forward still,
And lays his life down for his fellow man?

    O trust me, not in vain
    Our myriads of slain
Peopled the bosom of the inner earth;
    And not in vain the groans
Of those lamenting o'er their mouldering bones.
    Out of their ashes came
    A spirit all of flame,
A soul that gave our land another, better birth.
    The dead are our dead saints,
    Pure martyrs purged from taints,
    Who shaped with word and deed,
    Through storms of steel and fire,
    Through the torturer's fiendish ire,
    This nation's future creed.
    And the mourners shall remember,
    From green May to white December,
The lesson, growing clearer day by day;
    For so deep the brand of pain
    Stamped the thing on heart and brain,
It can never, never, never fade away!

    But take comfort, ye who weep
    For your heroes fast asleep—

Fast asleep, though gleams of glory
Flash a sunrise round their story;
  For, alas! on their dull eyes
  Neither sun nor star shall rise;
  And the rose of June in vain
  Shall scent the summer rain;
  And the trump and rattling drum
  In their stony ears are dumb;
  And the tenderest touch of love
  Cannot make their pulses move:
They shall never waken upon earth again!
  Their dwelling is not here,
  But behold them, shining clear,
  Where the war-worn soldiers all
  Pace God's celestial wall,
  When the evening turns to gold,
  And the vapors fold on fold
  Spread their banners in the west,
  And heaven's battlements are dressed
  With plumes and pennons gay,
As though the angels held a holiday.
  Then our heroes slowly glide,
  Soldier-like and side by side;
  To the ramparts on they move,
  And with eyes o'errun with love,
Gaze and gaze, in high angelic mood,
  On this world of ill and good,
  And to the passing ages tell
Their sentry watchword, "All is well!"
  O re-echo in their sight,
  From your hill-tops sunny height,
And the mellow swells and hollows of your lands,
The solemn greeting of their faithful bands?

Lift up your brightening face,
O enfranchised dusky race,
And show them your unshackled toiling hands!

Then let the steeples rock,
  And the belfries shake and quiver,
And the great bells clang and shock,
  And the small bells trill and shiver!
Let the smoking cannon boom,
  And the bending nation pray,
And the mourners' dreadful doom
  Lift its shadow for a day!
Let us turn a face joy-clear
  Unto heaven, with one accord,
And waft our victor's cheer
  Through our heroes to the Lord!
Bless His name, rejoicing men,
  For the bloody conflict's close,
For good-will restored again,
  For the balm that heals our woes;
For the ocean white with sails,
  And the rivers dim with steam,
For the humble world that quails
  At our flag's triumphant gleam;
For the bounty of His hand
  In the teeming fields' increase,
For the quiet in the land—
  For Union and Peace!

HYMN FOR THE UNION LEAGUE.

July 4, 1865.

THANK God! the bloody days are past,
Our patient hopes are crowned at last;
And sounds of bugle, drum and fife
But lead our heroes home from strife!

Thank God, there beams o'er land and sea
Our blazing star of victory;
And everywhere, from main to main,
The old flag flies, and rules again!

Thank God, O dark and trodden race,
Your Lord no longer veils his face;
But through the clouds and woes of fight
Shines on your souls a better light!

Thank God, we see on every hand
Breast-high the ripening grain-crops stand,
The orchards bend, the herds increase;—
But O thank God, thank God, for Peace!

SONNET.

RATHER, my people, let thy youths parade
    Their woolly flocks before the rising sun;
  With curds and oat-cakes, when their work is
    done,
By frugal handmaids let the board be laid;
Let them refresh their vigor in the shade,
    Or deem their straw as down to lie upon,
    Ere the great nation which our sires begun
    Be rent asunder by hell's minion, Trade!
If jarring interests and the greed of gold,
    The corn-rick's envy of the minéd hill,
    The steamer's grudge against the spindle's skill—
If things so mean our country's fate can mould—
    O let me hear again the shepherds trill
    Their reedy music to the drowsing fold!

www.ingramcontent.com/pod-product-compliance
Lightning Source LLC
Chambersburg PA
CBHW031739230426
43669CB00007B/411